MW00893908

WALKING
IN YOUR
DESTINY

BUILDING FAITH THAT CAN
MOVE MOUNTAINS

KATHLEEN MAILER

WESLEY
HOPKINS

Copyright © 2018

ISBN: 978-1-897054-93-2

Published by: Aurora Publishing – a Division of: Doing Business God's Way International Inc.

Produced by: ChristianAuthorsGetPaid.com

Walking in Your Destiny, Building Faith That Can Move Mountains

Compiled by Kathleen D. Mailer

Edited by: Ruth Yesmaniski & Cheryl Regier

No part of this publication may be reproduced, stored in a retrieval system, or transmitted in any form or by any means, electronic, mechanical, photocopying, recording or otherwise, without the written permission of the publisher.

The publisher gratefully acknowledges the many publishers and individuals who granted our *Walking in Your Destiny™* team the permission to reprint the cited material. Each author keeps the copyright for their own chapter in the book; to use at their discretion and will (alongside the publisher).

DISCLAIMER: Each author is writing from her own viewpoint, and it does not necessarily reflect the viewpoint of each heart that reads it. The reader cannot hold the publisher, compiler, editors, or any other members of the team accountable for any outcomes or conclusions they come to as they read this book.

Dedication

This book is dedicated to the extraordinary men and women that came to this year's *'A Book Is Never A Book'* Boot Camp! (www.ABookIsNeverABook.com)

What a privilege it is to walk alongside such great, talented individuals that are dedicated to seeing His Kingdom come!

Your devotion to our Lord, Jesus Christ, is MOST inspiring to watch! The anticipation always cultivates a mountain moving faith, as He begins to unravel the hidden treasures within the walls of your heart. We are left mesmerized as he begins to bring your destiny into fruition while His plans and purposes unfold before our very eyes.

We pray that this book becomes a tool to cultivate an 'I CAN' mentality as you step into the next level of faith. The faith that God would bring provision in the next season of your life; provision of time, finances, team members, and a resounding "YES" or "NO" from Holy Spirit – in answer to where you are to take the next step in your journey.

Love and blessings, now and forever...

Dan and Kathleen Mailer

Table of Contents

Acknowledgements

My heart is overwhelmed at the love and support of those people that make Boot Camp AND Walking In Your Destiny ™ possible!

Dan and I want to reach out and lift up to you, our incredible Walking In Your Destiny™ team. Saying 'thank you' doesn't even come close to expressing our heart-felt appreciation for your dedication and hard work to push toward our united goal. Seeing this book get into the hands of the people that God wants to encourage, strengthen, and transform is a dream come true. Helping others to birth their book into a hurting world is what we do, but without you – it could not be done.

To our editing team, Ruth Yesmaniski and Cheryl Regier, you are beyond gifted in the world of making sure our thoughts and ideas have a clear and concise target. Without your expertise and Holy Spirit guided gift, this book would not reach the intended person's heart. Our prayer for the both of you, is that God would bless the work of your hands and this year, your destinies to be Kingdom Wealth Creators would have you building your businesses upon the rock at a faster, consistent momentum. Health, wealth and happiness are a by-product of being heirs to the King! May you experience much more than you ever have in years gone by.

Partnering with you both has been such an incredible, God-ordained journey. THANK YOU!

Dan Mailer, oh my goodness, writing these words brings tears to my eyes as I search my heart for the words to express my sincere gratefulness for what you bring to our business (and to my life.) You are always 100%, full on 'in'. Your love for our Heavenly Father is prevalent in our 'family' business ministry.

Thank you for doing what I can't. Thank you for encouraging me to do what I can. Thank you for praying with me as we reach out to the Father – for Him to do, what HE does.

Of course, there are others who are always there to help me manage the room; coach those who are on-line and in person. Our grads who have walked the walk of publishing their own books – who feel called to give to others who are sitting in the chairs. Thank you for welcoming our new family members and continuing to support them even PAST the days of the Boot Camp! Being able to lean on you – has been one of the most humbling experiences of my life. Thank you – for being so kind and generous to both Dan and I and spilling over to all that you come into contact with. This also goes out to all of those who could not be here, with us LIVE at Boot Camp this year, but who have continued to intercede and pray for each author, and every book that is filled with the power of God's testimony.

You all know who you are, and Dan and I will always be eternally grateful for your generosity and gifting.

Of course, we would be remiss if we didn't take a moment to thank our graduating class of 2018 for an incredible book. Many of you have come from around the world to attend our Boot Camp. We are so proud of you for answering the 'call' on your life and taking steps of great faith to get to Boot Camp. May God bless you beyond your wildest imaginations? Without you, this devotional would not be this incredible tool for others to read and grow by. Without you, there would be no book or company – (ChristianAuthorsGetPaid.com) ... without you, we could not fulfill our own destiny. YOU are our family and we love you. We thank God for you – and your willingness to partner with us, as we go beyond our current ability to 'see' before us.

You encourage us to come alive and wake up every day determined to follow Jesus in a fresh and inviting way. YOU give us the courage to keep going when the enemy sends his storms. Thank you!

Last, but <u>NEVER LEAST</u>, always *first* in our lives...

Jesus, you who have laid down your life for us, there is nothing that we could say or do to thank you for your blood, sweat, tears, pierced hands, beaten, bruised and tortured body. Nothing can compare to what you have done for us. We can only offer you our lives as a living sacrifice and we look forward to the day – when we can meet you face to face to hear those precious words, 'well done my good and faithful servant'. How we long to be faithful and good for you!

*Holy Spirit...*year after year you promise that you will bring a greater glory than the year before, and... year after year, you blow our minds. Trusting in you is easy. Knowing you better and better is truly our pleasure. Partnering with you has been more than we could have ever hoped for. Thank you – for being forever there for us as we grow in our business ministry as Kingdom Wealth Creators, and in our life.

Father, Daddy, how much you care for this family of yours. We are truly honoured and privileged that you called us to lead with purpose, passion, power and profit in this revelation economy. These sisters and brothers you gather together take our breath away. Thank you for loving us unconditionally and helping us to grow to become the grown-ups you could be proud of. We are MOST appreciative to You, our wonderful God in all Your majesty and are indebted to Your goodness now and forever more.

Climb The Ladder of Faith

~KATHLEEN MAILER~

I would like you to take a moment to search your memory for a time that you recall seeing or hearing stories of a strong and capable body builder.

Think about the lean, focused definition of each muscle. How it sculpts the temple of God and transforms it into something of beauty.

This particular muscle brings strength, foundation, and balance to the CORE of this vessel.

Every fiber of it was built with several step-by-step, persistent and disciplined actions. It was built by flexing and stretching. Each movement required a succession of review plus movement forward into the next level of heavy lifting.

What happens with a body builder, when they decide not to push forward anymore with that laser beam focus on growth? Does their body continue to grow in strength and agility? OR, does their body – although it never totally weakens or goes back to the days before they decided to get into shape – lose their current level of strength on a slow and steady decline?

So, it is, with our faith ….

"Our FAITH is a muscle,

if you don't use it – you lose it."

-Kathleen D. Mailer

Scripture tells us, if we have faith the size of a mustard seed we can tell a mountain to move and it will! Nothing will be impossible for us. THAT is the kind of faith I am looking for in my life! How about you?

He replied, "Because you have so little faith. Truly I tell you, if you have faith as small as a mustard seed, you can say to this mountain, 'Move from here to there,' and it will move. Nothing will be impossible for you." Matthew 17:20 NIV

Everyone has been given the same measure of faith. (Romans 12:3-8). This means that we all have the same 'starting point'. Then why is it, in some areas of our life it feels like we are the one with 'so little faith?"

I pray, that the following thought points and illustrations will help you climb the ladder of faith – build a vessel with strong, balanced definition like the body builder we talked about it.

8

Let's take a moment to visit a few thought points shall we?

There are many areas of our life where we want to believe God for his incredible blessing, grace and favour. These regions in life can span all the way from finances; to health; to marriage; other relation-ships; into our ability to hear from Him; as well as, our own personal relationship with Jesus. (Just to name a few.)

Upon reflection, you will begin to see the fact that in some matters, (even that of your own salvation) you have UNSHAKEABLE FAITH. You trust that God will show up and provide in every way possible. It doesn't matter what obstacles that come up in that area – you know, that you KNOW – God is in control and the answers in which you seek from Him will come.

Isn't this truth?

Alternately, there may be one or two realms that you are crying out to God for breakthrough. You want to break free from the undeniable shackles that seem to keep you stuck. The distance between the visions God gave you for your life and that of where you are currently walking seems like a highly implausible ambition. It also seems that no matter

9

how hard you try; no matter how many 'prophetic words' you get about your destiny – you just CAN NOT seem to wrap your mind around (or have FAITH in) the undisputed fact that God WILL come through with His promises.

I know just how you feel! It is astonishing how many individuals come to Dan and I at this very junction in their life, for prayer. They are so discouraged, and they build up such condemnation and shame around their own conviction that 'they have so little faith.'

This shame and guilt become a great, gapping, gorge between them and their Father in Heaven. He is not the one that is condemning them – or saying, 'shame on you!' NO- THAT is NOT our Heavenly Father. That is the father of all lies... satan himself. (Please note, I never put a capital 's' on the devil's name – because he doesn't deserve that much attention!)

If this is you, I want to encourage you to get before the throne of grace before you finish reading this chapter. Ask for forgiveness for the way you have been treating yourself. For the way, you have abusively been cursing yourself, pushing yourself...

Once you have received his mercy, grace and forgiveness – stay in this place of prayer. Stand before God and the cloud of witnesses and say out loud –

"I forgive myself, in the grace and mercy that Jesus taught me, for carrying around this shame and guilt in the past. I let it go now, in the name of Jesus!" Amen.

Settle in your heart, once and for all, what area of life do you need to build your faith muscle? The truth is THAT arena is most likely the domain that your destiny call is hinged to.

Now that you are armed with these pertinent thoughts, let's get ready to go into training. It is time for you to be a *MASTER of UNSHAKABLE FAITH* as you piece together each of the action steps I share below.

Let's use our imaginations once again – as we begin to illustrate the way to build confidence and conviction in your dedicated allegiance to Jesus.

Envision, just ahead of you is a mountain with the longest ladder you have ever seen attached to it.

At the base of the ladder –where you currently stand - you find yourself weak, and your knees are knocking. You have no confidence in your ability to reach the top of the promise even though God, himself, has given it to you. You are frustrated because you want the promise RIGHT NOW! Why? Because you KNOW that you KNOW it is your destiny! You have tried everything you can think of, but the obstacle (mountain) doesn't seem to be budging.

These 7 Steps I share are by no means the entire plan to receiving great clarity and assurance in God, yourself and your abilities. However, it is a well-rounded way to begin your new 'workout regime' to build the strength you need to conquer unbelief.

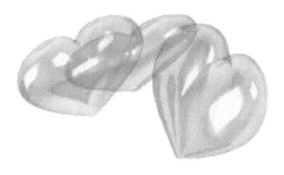

Climb the Ladder of Faith in 7 Steps

By Kathleen D. Mailer

Step One: **The WORD of God**

So faith comes from hearing, that is, hearing the Good News about Christ. Romans 10:17 NLT

Finding His promises and getting to know His ways helps build our faith in all ways.

Pour over scripture, read it daily. Find the passages that pertain to you, in this season you find yourself in right now. Declare and decree the WORD in, around and through your life. Remind yourself everyday what God has to say about the situation.

Our God is so good, his words will not return void! (Isaiah 55:11)

Step Two: **The TESTIMONY of Others**

The same scripture applies to the testimony of others who have found faith rooted in Christ Jesus.

There is great power in our testimony. If you think about it, the bible is filled with testimony, after testimony - and revelation upon revelation of who Jesus is!

One word of caution, there are always those – for reasons that protrude from their own experiences and observations – who will share a testimony of defeat, or distraction, or fear. What we listen to matters.

Find and receive the testimony of the Lord Jesus from those who are encouraging and equipping. Test the spirits (as the Lord leads – John 1: 4-6) to see if this testimony set before you is actually helping you to get closer to the prophecy the Lord put before you OR if it is keeping you grounded on the 'rung of the ladder' you currently are standing.

Step Three: **Write down and read what God has done for you!**

The devil is such a liar. He will have you believing that you have not had ANY growth in your life and he will try and pull the blinders over your eyes.

Your own testimony makes all of the difference in the world. When you get discouraged you can be reminded that God is with you, HE will see to it that you are taken care of. I love the following Psalm of

David - write your own Psalm of Triumph as a "remembrance" to keep Jesus in the forefront of your life.

The LORD Is My Shepherd (ESV Psalm 23: 1-6)

A Psalm of David.

23 The LORD is my shepherd; I shall not want.
2 He makes me lie down in green pastures.
He leads me beside still waters.
3 He restores my soul.
He leads me in paths of righteousness
*   for his name's sake.*

4 Even though I walk through the valley of the shadow of death,
*   I will fear no evil,*
for you are with me;
*   your rod and your staff,*
*   they comfort me.*

5 You prepare a table before me
*   in the presence of my enemies;*
you anoint my head with oil;
*   my cup overflows.*

*⁶ Surely goodness and mercy shall follow me
    all the days of my life,
and I shall dwell in the house of the LORD
    forever.*

Step Four: **Hang out with people who have MORE capacity faith than you currently do.**

As iron sharpens iron, so one person

sharpens another. Proverbs 27: 17 NIV

There is such a powerful place in the body of Christ when you have unity in your community. As Kingdom Wealth Creators, finding the right community is vital to your growth in faith as it pertains to fulfilling one's purpose.

Dan and I have experienced being in a community where there wasn't unity, with the trinity, with one another, or within individuals themselves. This will only bring down your faith levels and cause you to want to 'hide' instead of shine.

However, we have an incredible community of Kingdom Wealth Creators that have decided to take their message to the masses. They do it through their business ministry; writing and publishing books; speaking up and speaking out; and serving as best as they can for the glory of God.

Being around them inspires me to go deeper in my walk with Christ; motivates me to take action; and brings me hope – in every situation we face. This

'family' of ours (that God has graciously LET us lead) helps us to know we are not in this fight alone. We have each other.

Iron sharpens irons – is an incredible, awe inspiring way to build mountain moving faith.

Step Five: **Learn things.**

Let the wise hear and increase in learning,

and the one who understands obtain guidance,

Proverbs 1:5 ESV

Strength and understanding goes hand in hand. Finding mentorship and guidance in the tangible things of the promise of God is so valuable.

A great example of this is in this very book that you hold in your hands today.

Many of the students that come to our, 'A Book Is Never A Book Boot Camp" – come with very little faith that they too, could write a book. As a matter of fact, most are starting with a small seed, "God has called me to do write a book." They have absolutely no awareness of process to get their words on paper or in publishing or in the marketing - let alone HOW it fits into the puzzle of the purpose God has for their life!

Through the power of the Holy Spirit and the tangible workings of a 'how to…' scenario – together we built this incredible resource that you are reading this very day! Learning how to – takes you to the next rung as you climb the ladder of GREAT FAITH.

Step Six: **Plan things**

For which of you, desiring to build a tower,

does not first sit down and count the cost,

whether he has enough to complete it?

Luke 14:28 ESV

When one has a plan of actionable (action-able) steps the confidence in our abilities, and God's promises begin to grow exponentially.

However, one MUST take action and head the advice in scripture.

For as the body apart from the spirit is dead,

so also, faith apart from works is dead.

James 2:26 ESV

Step Seven: **Praise, Worship and Prayer**

As we began our climb, we stood on the WORD of God. As we come to a close, we will continue to climb higher by praising our King.

Worship takes you higher than you can imagine and opens the door for the supernatural favour of God to implode in your life.

Praising Him, who is worthy to be praised, will physically change your brain's processing unit and open up your perception of your current situation.

Praying that the Holy Spirit will be your teacher, comforter, and partner in this life – will inspire you to 'see' the next rung before you. Praying in the 'spirit' will open doors of opportunity, and close doors of deception or distraction around you.

Removing yourself from your current circumstances and sitting on our Father's knee gives you an 'over view' of the BIG picture so you don't get caught in the selfishness of 'it's all about me."

There is nothing that can compare to the one who is, who was, and who is to come, the Almighty God. (Rev. 1:8)

My prayer for you, in the words of our precious bible, *"May the God of hope fill you with all joy and peace as you trust in him, so that you may overflow with hope by the power of the Holy Spirit." Romans 15:13 NIV*

I trust that this book will bring you increased faith to conquer all fear and doubt that the enemy is trying to send you to STOP you from your inevitable success.

We would SO love to hear from you. If you feel led – don't hesitate to contact us or visit our websites.

Connect with our community of Kingdom Wealth Creators – for Facebook and Instagram, go now to: @KathleenAndDanMailer; OR, tweet with us on Twitter: @KathleenAndDan

Let me leave you with one last quote:

"Faith activates Hope - Hope spurs us into action!"
Kathleen D. Mailer

www.KathleenAndDanMailer.com
www.ChristianAuthorsGetPaid.com

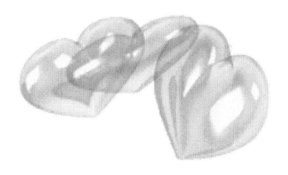

Faith

Prayer Building Faith

~TRUDY ASHER~

When I accepted Jesus as my Lord and Savior, I knew I needed to know how to pray. I bought every book I could find on the subject – ones on intercessory prayer, prayers to heal the sick, and others. In particular, I needed God to show me the secret things that were holding me back from my blessings and why finances had always been an issue in my life.

God reminded me of a couple of key Scriptures:

"Behold I am the Lord, the God of all flesh; is there anything too difficult for Me?" (Jeremiah 22:27, AMP)

'Call to Me and I will answer you, and tell you [and even show you] great and mighty things, [things which have been confined and hidden], which you do not know and understand and cannot distinguish.' (Jeremiah 33:3, AMP)

I needed answers. God's Word promised that I could enquire of Him, and He would show me all that I had need of. Through prayer, I could receive His wisdom, direction, and provision.

Now, I had been saving for a mission trip to Jamaica when an unexpected expense swallowed up everything that I had diligently saved up. I thought my trip was over. I needed a miracle...and a big one at that!

Around this same time, our pastor challenged the congregation to forty nights of prayer. During this time, we would meet for two hours every evening for prayer and worship. Each night, we were given an assignment to carry out. The focus of the first few days of prayer and their assignments really spoke to where I was at and the questions I had before the Lord.

The first evening, we were asked to write down every lost blessing that we could think of that we had personally experienced. Then, we were instructed to enquire of the Lord for the reasons why these lost blessings had happened or were happening. We were to petition the Lord: "Show me the secret" and "Show me my position in this battle". In addition, we were to ask the Lord to show us how to get back everything that had fallen out of our hands.

I wrote in my journal "DELVE". To delve means to dig or excavate, to investigate for information, to search for. I asked the Lord to delve into and root out any unhealthy "plant" or "weed" (sin) that had a stronghold in my life and expose every hidden thing that was not of Him – to dig deep.

The second night, we were asked to read Psalm 23 out loud three times a day. Interestingly, this passage is all about the Lord's provision. As part of our standing on this Psalm, we were to very specifically state that we would dwell in the house of the Lord forever.

The third night, we were taught on making decrees, quoting from this passage:

*"You will also decide and **decree** a thing, and it will be established for you; And the light [of God's favor] will shine upon your ways."* (Job 22:28, AMP; emphasis mine)

Then, our assignment that evening was to declare and decree the following:

• All heaviness that tries to oppress me and weigh me down, I reject you! I will arise and go forth in the name of the Lord!

- The Lord is the glory and the lifter of my head!
- My mind, will, and emotions will come in line with the Word of God, so arise now!
- I will hear the Lord this day!
- I will be guided in everything I do by the LORD'S direction, and I will follow!
- I expect and will receive good news today!
- I expect good changes in my life today!
- I am a magnet for good news, and good news will stick to me!
- I expect a financial blessing today!
- Let the breath of God breathe life into these words now!
- Captain of the Lord's army arise and fight for me today!
- All my blessings and lost opportunities come forth in Jesus' name!

I spoke these decrees again before going to bed that night and first thing the next morning as well. Little did I know that God was about to do something so profound in response! His answering came in a way that only He could do.

At 5:50 a.m., I made a note in my journal with a final decree, "I expect a financial blessing today, for I am a magnet for good news." Soon afterwards, my phone rang at 6:10 a.m. with a friend on the other end saying, "Trudy, what time do you leave for work today?" I told her that I was leaving at 7:45 a.m. She then went on to say, "The Lord woke me at 5:50 this morning and told me I am to bring something to you right away." She lived at the other end of the city and arrived approximately thirty minutes later. Handing me an envelope, she gave me a quick hug and said, "Have a blessed day!" Then, she turned around and left.

When I opened the envelope, inside was a cheque for $1000.00! Along with that cheque was a $100.00 bill with a note saying: "The tithe on the $1000.00." Plus, there was a $10.00 bill to be used as tithe on the $100.00 with another note stating: "But you need to supply the $1.00 tithe on this $10!"

I couldn't believe it! Who gives a tithe on a tithe? I'd never heard of anyone ever doing such a thing! And a cheque for $1000.00? This unexpected financial blessing was so unbelievable! Only God could have woken my friend up and told her to do this. This initial blessing was only the beginning of what God was going to provide for me.

God continued to add to my blessing for the rest of the month. When my family and friends heard the news of what had happened, they couldn't believe it either. They started sending me money to add to the blessing. I had money left on my chair at church. Money arrived in the mail. Colleagues from work blessed me with finances. In the end, I not only had my flight and all my expenses covered for the mission trip, I had extra left over to bless the families I would be ministering to while there. What a Mighty God we serve!

Through my obedience in prayer before the Lord, my faith was built up. As a result of this amazing encounter with God, I learned that all we have to do is believe that He provides for our every need, and He will do so even in unexpected and miraculous ways. He loves to bless His children!

If the Lord can do it then, He will *surely* do it again!

Trudy Asher lives passionately and purposefully for Jesus, taking joy in being a positive influence for those around her. Trudy is an author, having published and received the Editor's Choice Award for her poems "Reflection of God" and "Prayer of Love" by the International Library of Poetry.

Her up coming book is titled *Into Me I See*.

Health, Healing, Hope

~BEV BURTON~

My journey started in January of 2016 with the Doctor's diagnosis of the dreaded "C" word. I immediately went into denial, then anger, finally settling into my default "control issues". I was not going to tell anyone about the diagnosis, until common sense entered my thought process. I knew my family and close friends would find out when I went for surgery. Thankfully, I contacted my daughter and sister, asking them to attend the consultation appointments with their listening ears. I found myself totally blocking anything I did not want to hear. My daughter watched me during these appointments and could tell when I shut down, so she would take over. She was present for all the doctor's consultations and treatment appointments, ensuring no questions or areas of uncertainty were missed, also ensuring that everyone had the updated and correct information at the appropriate times.

Once it was determined that surgery was necessary, I felt I was still in control, having everything planned out as to what would happen after the surgery. God however had other plans! My surgery date was changed 3 times before I would give up control, releasing everything to Him. Two days before surgery, during my hospital admission appointment, I completely lost my cool. With anger and tears of frustration, knowing that I had no control of how the events would play out, my only way to peace was turning everything over to Him. Once I did this I was immediately filled with a sense of peace with the process. Giving up the control resulted in a speedy recovery along with a rapid healing process.

In June 2016, we arrived at the Cross-Cancer Centre for the follow up appointment. After the initial checkup from the surgery, discussions proceeded to the recommendation for chemotherapy and radiation treatments. Anger, denial and fear resurfaced again. I quickly made a very strong NO statement, that I was not going to take the treatments. We were encouraged to go and discuss the information about the treatment options returning in a couple of hours having made a decision. It was during this time that God spoke to me "It is not about you, but what I am doing in and through you!". I told my daughter and sister "I guess I am doing chemo and radiation", we returned with my new decision that was not made strictly on emotions as had happened in the first place.

I was majorly blessed because of this obedience in my faith journey, I was rewarded by the experience of going through chemo and radiation with minimal side effects. Over the next six months, my immune system was nonexistent, causing me to be aware while carefully eliminating the chances of catching a bug if I ventured out of my home. During this part of the journey, God was able to teach me through reading books, studying different areas of the Bible, listening to teachings online that took me deeper in my faith journey. I was also blessed to have many encouragers and people who supported me on my recovery journey in health and in faith.

January 2017 arrived, as difficult as it was and still is at times, to be patient - not following my plan but listening to God's guidance, - trusting that He knows the master plan for the rest of my life. I was given Psalm 23 to meditate on, and it has now become a part of my life, that the Lord is my Shepherd. What is a Shepherd? Someone who leads, feeds, protects his sheep, the sheep know his voice and will follow him where ever he goes. I am also reminded that I will lack nothing and be guided on the right narrow path not the wide fast highway. I do not need to fear the shadows and darkness, He will prepare a table before me in front of my enemies. The first 3 months were discerning months, then God had me make some major changes in my life as He took me to the next level of my faith journey.

I continue even today to read, study and glean whatever knowledge I come across, this process has taught me to study the Word and to research the information before taking it into my belief system. One of the main lessons I have learned is to take a short passage, even a single line; read it, reflect on the meaning; read it a second time, meditate on it, and read it for the third time. I was amazed at how my mind will recall it much easier beside the fact of gaining true understanding. It is also quicker to catch myself when my mind starts to wander, thinking of other things, then realizing I do not have a clue what I just read. Today I am aware how important it is for my well-being to be fed spiritually and mentally along with physically.

There were times when I felt very peaceful and there were times when I was anxious while worry, shame and fear tried to rob, kill and steal my joy. In this season I learned that the more I pushed forward the more persistent the enemy became because he did not want me moving forward. I am amazed at the strength, courage and self confidence that has been showing up the last year. At times I do not realize what a change there has been and so I need to take the time occasionally to write down some of the experiences, to reflect for a short time about where I came from compared to where I am today.

One huge area of change is in how I live (my life style) today!!! Before my journey started I thought I had to work, bought things to make me feel good and ate out way too much. Today I realize it was because I did not know, trust or like who I was. I was a person that was always trying to create peace for everyone else while experiencing no peace myself. Today I have purged a lot of things that I no longer require. I have also lost 70 lbs in the last 3 years contributing to my increased self-esteem, love of self, and peace with who I am.

People are now telling me they see a special glow around me and even though I have not seen or feel this, I take their word for it. At the end of March 2018, I posted 2 pictures of myself that were side by side; WOW, it was amazing to see the difference. I continue to learn by reading the Bible, being part of a Monday to Friday morning prayer group, listening to sermons that teach living according to my faith walk, not the ways of the world. The sermon teaching topics are based on the Bible regarding Mastering Your Money, a 7-part series called *Grow Up Spiritually*, a 4 part series on the good news

Gospel ending with the Good New gospel of the Resurrection on Easter Sunday.

This journey of health and healing gives me hope for the future, I am excited to continue to spend each day studying the Word.

Words are seeds that are planted in others. I am thankful and blessed when I hear how the words that I speak and/or write have given encouragement and hope to others. I need to be reminded as I am writing this chapter how important my words are, how I may never know where they have or will bring a shining light of hope into the darkness for someone.

Bev Burton, Founder of Redwood Support Network, Volunteer with my faith communities, Co-Author of 2 previous *Walking in your Destiny* books, Author of soon-to-be-published *Create Your Calm Waters,* and *Arise Shine Daily Devotional,*

Making God the Centre of

Your Marriage

~CHRISTINA FRIESEN~

Just five years into our marriage, my husband and I were struggling. Trying to communicate our feelings to one another **left each of us feeling like we were under attack**. No matter how hard we tried, it felt like we were speaking different languages. We spent most of our time talking over each other – trying to be heard instead of listening to what the other had to say. This, in turn, resulted in all kinds of misunderstandings and hurt feelings. Pride was definitely a huge, contributing factor to our communication issues as well. Our relationship was this never-ending tug of war.

Struggling with feeling inadequate, we never felt good enough for one another. It didn't help that, during arguments, we often picked each other apart by pointing out each other's faults. The focus was usually on how the other person needed to change and on what they were doing wrong. I honestly believed that he only remained married to me out of a sense of duty and not because he loved me. Deep inside, I wanted him to be proud of me and be proud to be my husband. Instead, I was convinced that he was disappointed in me.

Another problem we had was that we allowed too many distractions into our lives rather than making our marriage a priority. More often than not, we were consumed with work, family, and other obligations. Our marriage would get whatever little time was left over, resulting in the relationship not getting the energy or focus that it needed. When we did manage to squeeze time in for each other, we would be too tired or stressed to enjoy it. Our relationship was not getting the proper attention it required to thrive.

Attempting to fix our marriage, we tried many things on our own. We read books about communication, we struggled to learn each other's love language, and we made efforts to start complimenting each other and show our appreciation for each other. We also tried spending more quality time together. Unfortunately, any attempts to do the right thing felt more like we were just going through the motions. Our efforts weren't genuine. Therefore, no matter what we tried, we would always end up reverting back to the same, old, negative behaviours.

As a result, deep wounds formed, making it more and more difficult to heal or experience real growth and lasting improvement in our marriage. Over time, we began to put up walls, our hearts hardening towards one another. A sense of loneliness and despair crept in.

Then, all of a sudden, everything came to a head.

Feeling so overwhelmed and alone, I became desperate to just get away. I left a note one day that said: "I can't take the pain anymore. I'm sorry. Love Christina." I packed my bags and started to drive. I wasn't even sure what this all meant myself. I just knew I had to get away for a while.

While I was away, we both had time to really think long and hard about some things. I'm so thankful that my husband never gave up on me during this time apart, despite the fact that we were both so lost. Six weeks later, my husband flew out to meet me, and we drove back home together.

It was shortly after this that we came to realize what was missing in our marriage. It was *God*. We had been trying to fix things all by ourselves, in our own strength. It just wasn't working. Instead, we needed to be intentional about making God the centre of our marriage.

Inviting God into our relationship, our efforts took on a different approach. We started to study the Bible together every morning. We also made a point of sharing things with each other that we were grateful for at the beginning of each day, setting a positive tone for the rest of the day. As new struggles came our way, we would pray about them. Before bed every night, we would pray together about our thoughts and concerns, asking for forgiveness and giving thanks. Asking God to help us to become better spouses to one another, our focus shifted to how we could serve Him by serving each other. These are all things that we continue to do today. When our focus shifted to making God a part of our relationship, including what we could do for each other and how we could improve ourselves, our marriage began to transform in huge ways.

Through building our faith and making it the centre of our lives, our relationship saw real changes. Our communication was more effective, and we learned to listen to each other better. As we affirmed one another, we began to feel proud of each other. This made me want to be an even better wife to him and him to want to be a better husband to me. A stronger bond formed between us, and as a result, a deeper love for one another also emerged. Our relationship with each other grew immensely along with our relationship with God.

In the past after arguments, I would often experience hurt, holding on to those feelings for days and letting my emotions fester inside of me. I'd let those offences take over and distract me from everything else. I was so focused on what was said or done to hurt me that I couldn't see my part in things. I struggled to extend forgiveness or show my husband grace.

> *For if you forgive other people when they sin against you, your heavenly Father will also forgive you. But if you do not forgive others their sins, your Father will not forgive your sins.* (Matthew 6:14-15, NIV)

As we pursued our faith, we both learned how to show each other more grace, especially through forgiveness. Sometimes, we just had moments of weakness, but we came to realize that we were not each other's enemy. For myself, I've had to learn how to extend forgiveness more readily and not hang on to offences that may come. In the end, offering forgiveness helps me as much as it does my husband. Plus, forgiveness also has a way of diffusing things and bringing about healing. This grace through forgiveness was key to building our marriage up and turning it around.

Having balance in our lives is an area we've really focused on. Spending more time growing in our walk with the Lord has been a significant part of practicing balance in our lives. Taking time to be alone – having time to ourselves – as well as to be with each other as a couple has been an extremely important part of that. We've formed relationships with other Christian couples and now have a fulfilling social life. Quality time with family has also been an essential part of establishing balance in our lives. Doing ministry work together and helping the needy is a fulfilling way we spend time together. When it comes to our everyday responsibilities, we both share in taking care of those. Our life is not always perfectly balanced, but we are intentional about having a healthy balance in our lives and redirecting ourselves when necessary. Balance in our lives has given us a greater sense of accomplishment and a sense of peace.

> *Love is patient, love is kind. It does not envy, it does not boast, it is not proud. It does not dishonor others, it is not self-seeking, it is not easily angered, it keeps no record of wrongs. Love does not delight in*

evil but rejoices with the truth. It always protects, always trusts, always hopes, always perseveres. (1 Corinthians 13:4-7, NIV)

God has shown us through our walk of faith and in His Word what He really intends our relationship to be like. In the process, we have discovered what a huge opportunity it is to serve Him by serving one another. Making God the centre of our lives has made all the difference, allowing us to create a marriage that is loving, fulfilled, and purposeful. Building faith has resulted in a rebuilt marriage!

Christina Friesen is a published Author from Steinbach, Manitoba, Canada, Wife to a loving husband, and Mother of five (3 sons/2 stepsons). She is a long-distance, truck driver who enjoys doing ministry work. Her upcoming book is titled *Once Broken*.

Faith

Faith In Action

~JAMES FRIESEN~

My story began with a small step of faith-giving and trusting God.

It was during the Christmas season of 2013 when my wife and I decided to make "kits" for the homeless who we encountered on our long-distance trips hauling freight out of Texas to Canada. My wife researched the needs of the homeless and packed cloth bags filled with socks, hygiene products, water, a fast food gift card and a Bible. My wife was the inspiration and felt called to help the homeless but although I supported the idea, I was not as enthusiastic about it.....until I handed out my first bag.

As we drove through McAllen Texas, I noticed a lady at a traffic light begging for help. I stopped, and we called her over. As she approached our truck, it was then that I observed she only had one arm. I reached down from my window and gave her one of the bags we had prepared. I had no idea what an impact this would have on the lady, and especially on me! This lady was so thankful, with tears in her eyes she called me an Angel. This encounter truly impacted both myself and my wife.

We began to do more to help the homeless year-round and my wife started searching out and following other homeless ministries on Facebook. On one of these searches, she came across a man named Bobby who is a street minister to the homeless.

Bobby was born to a prostitute and never knew his father. He was trafficked as a child in a sex trafficking ring from which he later escaped as a youth along with some other victims. Without a family or any formal education, he turned to living on the streets. While on the streets and homeless, he turned to crime for survival as well as to support his acquired drug habit. He ended up contracting AIDS as a result of his drug use.

He spent most of his life on the streets, homeless, but after being on the streets for over 20 years, he gave his life to Jesus. This happened one night when he finally hit rock bottom. A huge storm washed out his homeless camp, leaving him drenched and cold. He was angry with God, he cussed at God, and began to blame Him for all the suffering and hardships in his life. This went on for about 20 minutes before he began to feel bad and have remorse for what he said. He then realized that *he* had been the cause of a lot of his own suffering and that he had hurt other people. He truly felt sorry for what he had done.

At that point, Bobby cried out to God and asked Him if He could free him from the slavery of drugs, that he would be ever-so-thankful.

To take shelter, he grabbed a bunch of newspapers from a nearby stand, climbed into a dumpster and covered himself with them. He then cried himself to sleep. The next morning, he woke up with an eye infection and knew he needed to seek medical attention quickly. He went to go find his friend Chris who was a nearby parking valet to ask for some change in order to get to the hospital.

While he was asking Chris for this emergency money, he heard a voice from behind him say "No! Don't do that!"

He turned around to see who could be saying such a cruel thing but to his surprise, he saw a famous football player standing there holding out a $100 bill for him. He was so excited that this famous person was helping him that he didn't realize that this was the beginning of God answering his prayer.

When Bobby was treated at the hospital, he found out that he would be permanently blind in that one affected eye. While staying at the hospital, the staff informed him that he would qualify for disability. They helped him fill out the forms but told him it could be a long process. Three weeks later, while Bobby was being released from the hospital, he was surprised to find out that he had already been approved for disability. (This is almost unheard of!) Although that was exciting news for Bobby, he doubted anyone would rent a place to him. He had no work references, no personal references and no prior rental references. Who in the world was going to rent to him?

Despite his doubt, he went to the first place to apply for an apartment rental. He was shocked when they approved him right away! After getting the keys and opening the door to his new apartment, Bobby realized that God had answered his prayer and was opening doors for him. Thank you, Jesus,!

He left his new home, went back to the alley, gathered up all his homeless friends and brought them back to his apartment. A local fire hall learned what Bobby had done and gathered a bunch of food and furniture to donate to them. This was the beginning of Bobby Depper's street ministry!

This man is an amazing example of faith in action. We followed him for some time watching his ministry and even watched live as he ministered.

Bobby lives by faith, he is entirely supported through gift cards, restaurant cards, and Visa gift cards. He has a small group of supporters, even so, sometimes he goes without food. However, he always gives and puts his faith in Jesus. He uses these cards to meet and feed the homeless and gives them the Gospel and a hand up. He knows how to get the help they need with ID and shelter information and works with local businesses to get them work.

One time he hadn't eaten for a day, so he searched his place and found an old Taco Bell card. He prayed there would be enough for a meal left on it and then he went to Taco Bell to eat.

As he was getting ready to order, a lady came up to him and said she had had nothing to eat in a while and asked if he could buy her some food. Bobby never says no nor did he this time, but then she said "I have two more friends that are hungry" and of course Bobby agreed to feed them as well. Bobby was now at the counter praying "Fish and loaves Jesus, fish and loaves." Miraculously, there was enough on the card for all of them to eat!

We witnessed Bobby giving his jacket to a shivering lady on the bus, going cold himself. I have seen him give the last of his money for food to a shoplifter. If Bobby sees someone shoplifting food, he stops them before they are caught and offers to pay for the food, which also gives him the chance to talk about Jesus.

Recently, through letters of commitment from various supporters, he was able to secure an apartment. This is solely on the promise of these people who give around $50 a month each, for a promised year of giving.

Bobby now had an apartment, but it was completely empty. Bobby's faith over many instances had inspired us to raise some money through an online garage sale, but we knew Bobby had many needs. We prayed with Bobby that night on a social media call with him in Oklahoma and my wife and I at home in Canada, for God to move hearts so that provision would come for a bed for him as well as for a few more needs.

The next day my wife paid for some pots and pans online for him to pick up at his local Walmart.

We sent Bobby to get them and being Bobby, as he got to Walmart on his bike, he saw some homeless people nearby, so he went to check on them, gave them some help and direction, and shared the Gospel with them.

Then he proceeded to get the pots and pans we bought him went on the way out, he noticed an older lady needing help with her bags. As he helped this lady, she mentioned that she saw him talking to the homeless people and was wondering what that was about.

Bobby shared his ministry story and how he got a new apartment. She found out that he had no furniture. She then stated that was no way for someone like him, who was spreading the Gospel and helping people, to live. She said "I have some friends. We'll stop by tomorrow and see what you need."

This lady happened to be friends with a Christian furniture store owner. She and her friends came by the next day and fully furnished his apartment with new couches, coffee tables, a kitchen table and chairs, beds, dressers and a microwave! Wow! He showed us a live video of his apartment. What an answer to prayer! What timing! What a move of Christian hearts!

God is able to do far more than we could ever ask or imagine. He does everything by his power that is working in us. (Eph 3:20, NIRV)

My faith has grown tremendously watching God answer our prayers and seeing Bobby's faith in action.

Bobby Depper is truly passionate about leading others to Christ and giving them a hand up.

If you feel led to help, you can support Bobby at:

https://www.gofundme.com/make-bobbys-dying-wish-come-true

Or you can contact Bobby Depper by email at: bobbydepp7@gmail.com

James Friesen is a long-haul truck driver and author of his soon to be published book, *"I Can Get Up From Here!"* First and foremost, he is husband to a beautiful wife and father of 2 sons and 3 stepsons and is also involved in ministry to the homeless.

Fight the Good Fight of Faith

~DR. DIANE GARDNER~

"Fight the good fight of faith, lay hold on eternal life, to which you were also called and have confessed the good confession in the presence of many witnesses." (1 Timothy 6:12, NKJV)

When asked by my pastor to memorize 1 Timothy 6:12, it didn't make sense to me. Isn't all fighting bad? I thought a "good" fight needed an attitude full of anger and unforgiveness. Also, suppose it isn't in your nature to fight. It certainly wasn't in mine that was for sure! Let me share how I embraced the truths found in this verse and how they changed my nature.

"You're out!" I yelled as Shirley slid into home base, and Rachel tagged her out. I was the softball referee and the one left in charge while our 9th grade, Physical Education (PE) teacher was in her office.

"No, I'm not!" she screamed as she advanced until we were nose to nose.

"What I say goes, and I said you're out!" I hollered back.

51

Shirley didn't back down. "Meet me at the back gate after school, and we'll settle this my way!" she demanded.

I put my hands on my hips and tried to sound as tough and confident as she had. "Sure! You bring your friends, and I'll be at the back gate with mine!" I retorted in return.

As soon as school was over that day, I darted out the front gate and ran home as fast as I could, leaving Shirley and her posse high and dry as they waited for me at the back gate.

Growing up in Los Angeles, California, it was nothing short of a miracle to be a 14-year-old who had never had a fight. It seemed like many kids were angry and wanting to fight anyone and everyone. But I had a system that worked for me. Even at home, I had a strategy. I had never been in a fight, not even with my three siblings. Oh, of course my sister and two brothers hit me, but I never hit them back for fear things could escalate into something ugly. Instead, I'd laugh at them and say, "Ha, that didn't hurt!" (even if I was in pain), or I yelled for whichever parent was closest.

The next day, I arrived at school a half hour earlier than usual and ran straight to the Vice Principal's office. He handled the school's discipline. I told him what happened and gave him a list of names, starting with Shirley's. I said they wanted to fight me, but he could count on me to never be in a fight.

Later that day, Shirley and a couple of her friends surrounded me in the hallway. They were livid because they said they had waited half an hour at the back gate, and I never showed up.

"Well, too bad for you for being so stupid!" I stated loudly. Then, I lowered my voice and said to her, "I don't want to fight you."

My foe was taller by about 3 inches. In response, she balled her fist and hit me on the top of my head.

Fortunately, I was in front of my English class where one of the meanest 4'10" teachers you would ever want to meet taught classes.

So, I did what any non-confrontational chicken would do. I screamed at the top of my lungs. "Ms. Duncan! Ms. Duncan!"

She bolted out of her classroom and yelled, "What's going on?"

I pointed at Shirley and then at her friends. "They want to fight me, and I never fight." Pointing back at Shirley, I exclaimed, "She started it!"

Ms. Duncan reached up and squeezed the nerve between Shirley's shoulder and neck, the one over her collarbone. She held her tightly as Shirley bent over and complained, "Ou-u-ch!" They marched to the Vice Principal's office where he had Shirley's name on his list.

Now, that is what I call a *good* fight...one where I never needed to land a blow.

My nature was to try and talk my way out of any situation or hide somewhere in our house when there was conflict. My parents argued continually, and that kept my nerves on constant edge. Consequently, I was fearful of conflict.

To this day, my sister loves telling the story of how I walked backwards for three miles – from the school all the way to our house – while I tried to convince a friend not to fight me over a misunderstanding.

After close to an hour, my sister couldn't take my chicken feathers anymore. She ran home to our mom who had walked in the door from work expecting to see her four children already there.

Barbara bolted through the door and told Mom what I was doing. She made sure Mom knew it was not her fault that we were late coming home.

Our mom had a quick solution to this dilemma. "Diane never wants to fight because she doesn't want to get hit. Here's what will solve everything. You go back there and hit Diane yourself, and the fight will be over, or [the other girl] will throw the second blow. Then, you guys get back here immediately."

Fortunately, by the time Barbara returned, I had talked my "friend" out of her anger. I was a block away from home.

Today, I am known as a courageous person – one who fights the Enemy immediately upon recognizing his tactics. I'm not moved by what I see. Instead, I move mountains of opposition with patience and perseverance. My emotions don't get to vote in a crisis; only the Holy Spirit and the Word of God are my counsel. My memories as recounted in my book, *Overcoming the Enemy's Storms,* reveal this. I hold Overcomers Conferences teaching others to have the mindset of an overcomer God's way.

What changed my nature from that of a chicken to that of an eagle?

At age 22, I asked Jesus Christ to be my Lord and Savior. I said I believed He was raised from the dead and is in Heaven. I asked for forgiveness from all I had done wrong and for all the things He didn't want in my life. I didn't feel anything, but the miracle of the new birth happened instantly.

Since becoming a believer, I have wanted to please God in my decisions. However, back then, I never thought He cared about whether I liked to fight...especially with Scriptures that told us to turn the other check.

I wondered why the Bible was filled with constant conflicts, battles, wars, and fights. The Word says that God is a God of Love and Jesus is the Prince of Peace. That being so, why was there so much violence in Scripture? Thinking about all this made me nervous. Not long after these questions arose in my heart, my answer came.

I heard a minister teach on Mark 11:23:

"For verily I say unto you, That whosoever shall say unto this mountain, Be thou removed, and be thou cast into the sea; and shall not doubt in his heart,

but shall believe that those things which he saith shall come to pass; he shall have whatsoever he saith." (KJV)

That sermon and this Scripture thoroughly captivated me. Wow! What authority! What power! All contained in that one verse!

In hearing this Scripture, I felt the yearning to express mountain-moving faith. Yet, at the same time, my heart – my nature – resisted the idea of fighting any type of fight. I felt the spiritual struggle.

As I sat on my couch and read through and meditated on that verse later, God spoke to my heart. From that day, I learned four, valuable, life lessons.

"Daughter, the mountain in Mark 11:23 represents an opposition which does not need to be in your life. You cannot have the results of Mark 11 and refuse 1 Timothy 6. You say that 1 Timothy 6:12 is against your nature. You tell Me you cannot and will not fight. It breaks My heart when you refuse to fight the good fight of faith. A good fight is one where you have an unfair advantage over your opponent."

Lesson 1: I was astonished to think that the God of the universe even cared whether I had the heart of a chicken or the heart of an eagle. Then, to know it broke His heart when I refused to acknowledge there was a daily battle from an opposing kingdom surprised me further.

God said, *"You have an Enemy who is a violent foe. He brought violence even to the first family when Cain killed his brother Abel. You will always have an Enemy whether you fight him or not. Satan will always oppose you because he opposes Me. My Son had to die a violent death, and blood had to be shed to overcome this violent Enemy.*

"And from the days of John the Baptist until now the kingdom of heaven suffers violence, and the violent take it by force." (Matthew 11:12, NKJV)

Lesson 2: I found out God's Enemy was alive and well on planet earth, and that makes him my Enemy also. I had a responsibility to take God's will to be done and His Kingdom to come to any person or situation.

"My child, your mouth speaks words of victory about mountain-moving faith. At the same time, your heart tells Me you don't want to fight. That makes you double-minded. Because of this, you won't be able to help yourself or anyone else. You are convinced that to fight is not in your nature. But

I say to you, with My help, that you can change your nature by a quality decision in a moment's time."

God went on to impress upon me: *"You were born with a will to win, but life has convinced you otherwise. Your family, coworkers, neighbors, the world, and even my angels are dependent on you to fight battles and win wars – not like the world does but by My Word."*

Lesson 3: To be double-minded is to sabotage our own faith. When I am double-minded, I cannot receive anything from the Lord. Faith pleases God and has a direction. It is better to head in a direction listening and watching for further direction. I must choose to be a winner from my heart.

I got nervous, and that knot came back into my stomach. I didn't know how to respond. There was dead silence as He let me swallow this revelation.

Then God said: *"If you are going to move mountains, you must choose to have the attitude of a warrior, the mind of an overcomer, the courage that leads to victory, and the patience to outwit and outwait the Enemy."*

Lesson 4: To fight is not personality driven, but it's driven by our will. So, I can change my mind...and change my nature. God's Son acquired His seat in Heaven next to His Father by conquest, and I am a joint heir with Him. I spiritually sit on the same throne to rule and reign with Him.

I adopted Mark 11:23 as my life motto that day. I often say boldly, "I have mountain-moving faith! Nothing stands in my way!" Holy Spirit's teaching and my choice changed my nature to one of faith, even a faith that can move mountains.

Are you a chicken when it comes to fighting the good fight of faith? Or are you and eagle, soaring above all difficulties with mountain-moving faith? The choice is yours daily...moment by moment.

You CAN boldly declare, "I *have* mountain-moving faith. I *will* fight the good fight of faith. My heart and mouth are *in agreement* with God's Word because I was born to win!"

Dr. Diane Gardner, D. Div., is a speaker and best-selling author of *Increase Your Capacity to Hear From God: Stop Walking in Presumption* (2 editions), her popular memoir, *Overcoming the Enemy's Storms,* and a coaching manual: *You Can Be Healthy, Wealthy, and Wise*. She resides in Riverside, California, and can be reached at dianegardner.com.

Levelling the Enemy

~WESLEY E. HOPKINS~

For we cannot but speak the things which we have seen and heard. (Acts 4:20, KJV)

You have either entered into a mountain unknowingly or have purposed yourself to do so; either way the mountain must be moved out of your life in order to have freedom. We do so by first understanding our Authority in Christ.

It all started with experiencing the love of God for me, then His great mercy rang in, delivering me from the depths of this fallen world. I was lured into darkness at the age of 17 by alcohol and drugs. Over the next 22 years of my life the enemy totally controlled my every way of living. My life was destroyed and I lost my family. Between the ages of 36 to 38 I was lost deep in a dark organization, blinded from the truth. At the age of 38, the emissaries of that organization took me out of my house one night and into their "care" under the guise of a trial project they were testing.

One month later I was released and then at the age of 39, less than a year later, I was snared by the enemy as they sprang their final ploy to take my life and soul. (I will be going deeper and into much more detail on this in my first book that I am author and publisher of, which is set to launch early in 2019.)

The thief cometh not, but for to steal, and to kill, and to destroy: I am come that they might have life, and that they might have it more abundantly (John 10:10, KJV).

I assure you that the Lord Almighty is going to bring light to all the darkness I have experienced. The Lord gave me a vision of Him grinding the perpetrators into a fine powder.

And whosoever shall fall on this stone shall be broken: but on whomsoever it shall fall, it will grind him to powder. (Matthew 21:44, KJV)

In the meantime, let us move into some of the things the Lord has built into me out of my experiences so far, how He has used what was meant for evil and turned it into good.

Throughout my life journey there are many valuable things I have learnt, three in particular that I'd like to touch on are:

1) the Grace & Mercy of God

2) the Victory that is in Jesus

3) the truth about Truth.

I have personally experienced great depth in each of these, which has had the effect of rooting me deep into the Faith in the Lord's divine power which moves mountains.

I tell you the truth, you can say to this mountain, 'May you be lifted up and thrown into the sea,' and it will happen. But you must really believe it will happen and have no doubt in your heart. (Mark 11:23, NLT)

Jesus Christ saved my life and this is the only way and the only reason to why I am alive today to share this with you. From making nearly a six-figure income all the way to homelessness in a year, the Lord brought me out of what spiralled my demise. These are some of the consequences of what the enemy can and will do to you, when you don't conform to their demands. They will fabricate fictitious schemes against you and make you aware of them so that you know they may be able to frame you.

I say the truth in Christ, I lie not, my conscience also bearing me witness in the Holy Ghost, (Romans 9:1, KJV)

By the Lord's merciful deliverance, I was set free from being possessed and oppressed by evil spirits. If you have been involved with alcohol and/or drugs then I am confident that there are one or more evil spirits involved in one way or another in your life. In my case, alcoholism was a lie, because I was influenced directly by evil spirits. After much spiritual warfare I was completely delivered, meaning not only did the evil flee from within me but I was set free from "alcoholism". To this day I do not have any urges, cravings, desires or even a thought about drinking or doing drugs. This experience even exposes the deceptions within psychology because psychology will teach you that you cannot control a thought but will offer you many techniques and strategies to do so. These thoughts that they say you cannot control are from your soul realm and can only be totally controlled by either evil spirits (which you do not want – trust me!) or submitting yourself to the Lord (which is a taste of Heaven).

However, pulling your mind into the obedience of Christ is done simply by reading the living Word which is the Holy Bible and doing so every day.

Casting down imaginations, and every high thing that exalteth itself against the knowledge of God and bringing into captivity every thought to the obedience of Christ (2 Corinthians 10:5, KJV).

The fallen world we live in will not teach you the truths about life and the secular education system definitely will not!

Don't let anyone capture you with empty philosophies and high-sounding nonsense that come from human thinking and from the spiritual powers of this world, rather than from Christ. (Colossians 2:8, NLT)

This world is being run by unbelievably sinister and demented people who are being controlled by the Devil/Satan and his adherents. I was saved out of it all by the Grace and Mercy of God once I accepted Jesus into my life and heart.

For He has rescued us from the kingdom of darkness and transferred us into the Kingdom of his dear Son, who purchased our freedom and forgave our sins. (Colossians 1:13-14, NLT)

I live my new life dedicated each day to my Lord and Saviour Jesus Christ because of what He has done for me and my family. Father God has placed my family and I into His protective love, and just for that alone, I cry out with a thankful and grateful heart. Jesus is my all and everything, my friend and the lover of my soul. Over the last 2 years of my new life I have spent countless hours determined in study to know the truths about the Kingdom of God. Bible study after Bible study, Prayer after Prayer, battle after battle, conference after conference and much teaching from various Bible-believing churches, plus being in my third year of a Ministerial training school, I have joined King Jesus and His Kingdom to shake this world up to Truth and Justice! Knowledge is powerful and Truthful knowledge is Mountain Moving Power!

Blessed are they which are persecuted for righteousness' sake: for theirs is the kingdom of heaven. (Matthew 5:10, KJV)

We are enriched when we bear the wounds of being persecuted for doing what is right and truthful, for that is when you actually experience the Reign of Heaven's Kingdom. We are to establish the ways and Truths of God's Kingdom here on earth and in doing so we are actually Ruling and Reigning with

Christ. God's Government shall Rule and Reign here on earth, that legal right was given to our King at the Cross.

And having spoiled principalities and powers, he made a shew of them openly, triumphing over them in it. (Colossians 2:15, KJV)

Satan and all his evil followers were defeated at the Cross by Jesus atoning for all sin. Sin was the legal right Satan had to hold man in captivity and now that sin is atoned for, that legal right is no more, and the captive is set free from bondage to the Devil and the world.

We are to fight for position and overcome opposition and we do so by using the Word.

Think not that I am come to send peace on earth: I came not to send peace, but a sword. (Matthew 10:34, KJV)

The sword is the Word and the Word is Jesus and Jesus is Truth because it is actually against His very nature to be able to lie, He couldn't even if he tried. Evil of the hearts manifested once Jesus appeared on this earth and that in and of itself displays His power of righteousness. By this I mean we did not have anything to measure our hearts against until righteousness showed up, which is Jesus. We did not know our hearts were evil or at least not to the extent as we do now because Jesus draws it out of our hearts and then we either deal with it or ignore it – free choice is ours but woe unto the ones who ignore God Almighty. Allow the Lord to search and test your heart so that you can be right with God. This is so very important, and I will stress this point that it is _ALL_ about the matters of the heart with God.

Guard your heart above all else, for it determines the course of your life. Avoid all perverse talk; stay away from corrupt speech. (Proverbs 4:23-24, NLT)

Conflict and division are a certainty. When we move using the Word of God there is a manifestation of both Kingdoms where then we divide, round-up, separate the Kingdom of Darkness and bring it unto the Rule and Reign of the Kingdom of God. This world rightfully is dominated by our King and Lord Jesus Christ. We are to take back what was stolen from us in the Garden of Eden.

I give Jesus Christ All the glory and honor in all my ways.

Jesus, I Love You with all my Heart!

Wesley E. Hopkins, a published author, is united to and protected by the King and Lord Jesus Christ. I am currently working on my next book set to be released early next year.

Faith

In the Face of Fear

~LORRAINE JACYSZYN~

Red-faced, eyes dark with anger, the huge, German man roared, "I'm going to kill you!"

He lunged forward as if to carry out his threat.

I held up my phone and shouted at him, "I'm calling the police!"

His friend grabbed him by the arm and tugged at him, "Let's go," he urged, "before you do something you'll regret." Finally, his friend coaxed him to leave.

The whole confrontation started because my husband had agreed to let the German man rent the front of our shop for a showroom for his handcrafted furniture. Three months had already gone by, and he had not paid any rent. My husband confronted him and said that he would hold the furniture as collateral until he paid what he owed.

Of course, this made the man furious. That's why my husband and I found ourselves in such a precarious situation with this giant of a man threatening to kill us. The notion of police involvement seemed to take some of the wind out of his sails, and he finally left, cussing and deriding us vehemently.

"I'll make you pay for this!" he warned as he stomped out the door.

My husband and I let out a huge sigh of relief as he left. We were both feeling pretty rattled over the whole situation as neither one of us like conflict. Shaken, we decided to lock up the shop and go home.

Before leaving that day, we prayed for the Lord's protection over everything, for we had no idea what that crazy, angry man might do. We worried that he might try to break in to or burn down the shop. We were concerned that he might come to our house, which had us feeling apprehensive for the safety of our small children. We needed the Lord's protection!

That evening, as I continued to pray over the situation, God spoke to me, *"Lorraine, I want you to go and talk to that man."*

I argued, "Lord, I don't want to talk to him. Why don't you send my husband?"

Firmly, He replied, *"You are to go."*

I continued to argue, "That man threatened to kill me!"

"Do you remember Ananias of Damascus and Saul?" the Lord asked.

I cast around in my memory for the details of this story as recounted by Scripture and remembered vaguely that Ananias had been sent to heal Saul's eyes after Jesus had met Saul on the road to Damascus. At that time, Saul was zealous in his persecution of Christians, killing and jailing men, women, and children who had faith in Jesus. He had just convinced the Jewish authorities to allow him to widen his persecution by going to other cities and hunting Christians down. On the way to Damascus, Jesus met him in a blinding light. Following that encounter, Saul was blind for three days.

I thought I had better read the account in the Bible to get a clearer picture. I needed to see what the Lord meant when He asked me if I remembered Ananias and Saul. I opened my Bible to Acts Chapter 9 and read about the conversion of Saul. Ananias's words caught my attention.

"Lord," Ananias answered, "I have heard many reports about this man and all the harm he has done to your holy people in Jerusalem. And he has come

here with authority from the chief priests to arrest all who call on your name." (Acts 9:13, NIV)

Ananias was just as worried for his safety as I was for mine! He knew that Saul was a dangerous man and that he could be risking his life by obeying the Lord's command. Yet, even though Ananias initially argued with the Lord, he was faithful and obeyed. He went and laid hands on Saul's eyes, and Saul's eyes were opened.

In reading this story, I knew that I would have to obey the Lord as well – even if my life was on the line. I was terrified, but I had hope that, just as things turned out well for Ananias, this matter would turn out well for me, too.

I shared with my husband what the Lord had said to me and told him I was going to go and talk to the man. Surprisingly, my husband did not try to stop me. He just simply responded, "Do what you have to do."

Shaking, I got in to my vehicle and drove to the man's office, praying for the Lord's protection all the way. I had *no* idea what I was to say to him. The Lord wasn't giving me any clues. This step of obedience was nerve-wracking!

It was evening, and all the offices in that area where normally closed. I secretly hoped that he wouldn't be there...but I saw a light in the window. Timidly, I knocked on the door.

The door burst open, and the large man bellowed at me cursing and demanding why I was there.

"God sent me to talk to you," I managed to squeak out.

"You know I could grab you with one hand and choke the life out of you!" he uttered menacingly, towering over me in a very intimidating manner.

"I know," I said shakily, "but God has sent me, and He will protect me."

At that, he stood aside and beckoned me to come in. He led me to a small room off the hall and sat down in a chair by a small table. I sat down on the other side of the table. Gingerly, I looked at him, still wondering what the Lord wanted me to say to him.

Speaking up first, he began to share, "Everything has been falling to pieces – my business, my family, my health. I don't know what to do anymore. I'm at the end of my rope. I'm not a praying man, but last night, I was down on my knees, crying and asking

God to send someone to talk to me. In fact, I was very close to ending it all."

It was hard for me to imagine this arrogant man on his knees crying out to the Lord, but now I knew why I was there. He had asked for the Lord to send him someone to talk to him...and I was that someone!

Then, it was my turn to speak. I said, "You know, I wouldn't have come here on my own accord, but the Lord spoke to me and said that I must come and talk to you."

"After all the things I said to you," he replied gruffly, "I know you wouldn't want to be around me. It must be God!"

"Yes," I answered confidently. "God cares for you so much that He answered your prayer and sent me to tell you about Him. He sent you someone you would never expect to prove that He is God and heard your prayer."

I went on to ask him, "Have you heard about His Son, Jesus?"

Then, I proceeded to tell him about Jesus and why we need a Savior. Teary eyed, he agreed to pray with me and accept Jesus in his heart as his Lord and Savior.

"Now, I have hope that Jesus will help me," the repentant man whispered, wiping the tears off his cheeks.

After praying with him, I left. Thanking God for His protection, mercy, grace, and love for us lowly humans, I drove home. When I got home, I relayed all that had happened to my husband, and we rejoiced in the goodness of the Lord together.

I never saw the man again. He packed up and moved away, and I don't know what happened to him. However, I have confidence that Jesus is taking care of him still.

When I found myself in that frightening situation, it put my faith to the test. I literally had to decide to trust God whether I lived or died. My life was in His hands.

Not knowing what will happen but obeying God no matter what is important. Why? Because you never know what God has in mind! It turned out that this incident was a matter of spiritual life and death for that German man. If I had not come, he might have lost all hope and committed suicide as he had intended. Because I obeyed God, he is now spiritually alive in Jesus Christ. God demonstrated His sovereignty and great love by orchestrating our meeting. The end result grew my personal faith and ignited new faith in another.

This experience taught me three things:

1. Faith takes action in the face of uncertainty and fear.

2. God answers the cry of the heart and ministers to each of us individually to grow our faith. This demonstrates God's great love for everyone and the value He places on each one of us.

3. My faith in God's protection was elevated.

But let all who take refuge in you be glad; let them ever sing for joy. Spread your protection over them, that those who love your name may rejoice in you. (Psalm 5:11, NIV)

Lorraine Jacyszyn is the author of *Heart Echoes and Soul Wounds: Healing Through Poetry.* She is a busy mother of 12 marvelous children. Her heart is to equip and help others live victoriously in Christ.

Family Day(s)

~SUZANNE D. JUBB~

Lake Pelletier in Saskatchewan is a special place for our family. There has only been one summer that I have not made it to the lake. It was the perfect summer holiday. Waterskiing, tubing, paddle boating, fishing competitions, treasure hunting, hiking or running the hills, swimming to the other side of the lake, golfing, leech collecting, sun tanning, reading, cooking and cleaning with nephews and nieces, enjoying campfires and tenting were just some of the fun things we enjoyed. There were also conflicts, blessings and surprises that made 'the lake' the perfect setting for family building, and solidifying relationship ties.

One July day in about 2005, God awoke me at around 5 a.m. and I 'saw' scriptures of healing as if watching on a TV screen: the passages rolled by, one by one, like movie credits. By the time the last verse scrolled through, I knew in my heart that I needed to gather the family and pray for my mom that same day.

(Over the years, Mom had endured many health challenges. She had many operations which included back surgeries and open-heart surgery to name a few. Mom was often in varying degrees of pain which she bore without complaint.)

After supper, I suggested to all who were there that we pray together as a family, mindful of the reassurance of this Scripture: *Again, truly I tell you that if two of you on earth agree about anything they ask for, it will be done for them by my Father in heaven. For where two or three gather in my name, there am I with them. Matthew 18: 19-20(NIV)*

That evening, grandchildren and all, we prayed for Mom. You need to know that in my family this was not at all 'normal' practice, but on that very special, unanticipated day, we - grandchildren, nephews, nieces, brothers, sisters and everyone else that was there - all joined in. We thank you God, for we had Mom with us for another 12 years.

Fast-forward 12 years to Family Day weekend 2018. In Medicine Hat, while out for lunch with Dad after church on Sunday, February 17th, Mom suffered a stroke. Dad said his last words to her which were "Sweetheart, why aren't you eating?", after which she went silent and still. Soon after, she was taken to Foothills Hospital in Calgary, and in the next hours as the family arrived, we knew that we were there to spend our last time with her. Over the next four days, as we prepared ourselves and the family for the inevitable, words began to come. With God's help, I was able to imagine what might have passed between the Lord and our 'Mama Bear':

"GOD are you there?"

I AM. Right here. Always.

"Do you have time to chat?"

Of course, I do. Tell me your heart.

"I'm really tired."

I know; I see you, and I have been waiting, my Therese.

"Father - I have had a good life, and now I want to come home. I want to be with you and all of my loved ones."

You are ready. It is time.

"Father?"

Yes.

"I want to ask: can I be part of the planning?"

Of course, you can.

"Can I tell you what I need?"

Absolutely; I'm listening.

"Can you give them a little time to prepare their hearts?   I don't want them to be sad."

We can arrange that -sure.

"Father, family has always been so important to me and I do want to connect with as many of them as I can.   Can this happen over the Family Day weekend?"

Yes, yes! Good idea!

"How will it come to be?"

I have the perfect plan.

"Tell me more."

On Saturday, February 17th, you will enjoy your last hockey game with friends. On Sunday, I want you to go to church. After the Our Father, *close your eyes. You will see me wink. That will be my sign to you that the plan is under way. When mass is over, you will go to the restaurant and then your new journey will begin. You will have a stroke. Your family will come to realize that these are your final moments. You will not be able to speak.*

"I won't be able to speak? But FATHER...how will I connect?"

Therese, you have given selflessly over all these years. . . now it is time for you to be still, and to simply receive." Your family will be there; they will envelop you in their love.   Let them.   And even so, as you are growing faint, you will hear each and every word.   You and they will know that you are content.   I will give you this.

"But, Father, how will they *know* that I can hear them?"

When they speak to you, you will turn your head to receive their tender words. They will know. You will also have three tears. The first will fall on Family Day.

The second will fall when Aime tells you that he is taking you home.

The last tear will fall, when you speak to your sister Monique.

Not one tear will be wasted. They will be used to water the heavenly garden.

"Is there anything else, Lord?"

Yes...Remember that Mother's Day poem from many years ago? Remind them of it. They will want it for your eulogy.

"Father, I love your plan. One last thing: when I breathe my last, will you take my hand?"

You know I will. I have held it all these years and I will be holding it always.

And so, even through our grieving, we found comfort in Jesus's words:

I am the resurrection and the life. The one who believes in me will live, even though they die; and whoever lives by believing in me will never die. John 11:25-26 (NIV)

So Mom believed, so Mom lived, and so Mom *now* lives – and so we are at peace that she is now pain free.

One of what would prove to be several God incidences over those days would be a special moment that my son experienced. As he was sitting in his vehicle, suddenly – uncued – the song *Heaven's Garden* began to play from his phone. This was a song he knew would be part of the funeral services; he recalls a strong shiver going throughout his body at that moment, and so he decided to talk to Mom. I wasn't there, so I don't know what the actual conversation was, but I do know that there will be more 'Mom-and-God incidences' to watch for. Mom will be 'praying and doing' now, even as she did throughout our lives and to the end of her own.

From now on, Family Day in February will **not** be a sad day for our family, but rather a reminder of God's loving grace. He spoke to us all that week, gently and surely, through Mom, whom I know has *'...fought the good fight, finished the race and kept the faith.'* *2 Timothy 4:7-8 (NIV)*

Suzanne D Jubb Is the author of *The Golden Goose – One Important Step to Financial Freedom*. She is passionate about teaching. Her gift is her ability to simplify material so that all learners can benefit. She is also a proud mother and grandmother.

Faith

How Did That Happen?

~MARGIE MCINTYRE~

I had been offered a home, a safe place to live with people who came to love me. And I loved them! It was comfortable, a bit chaotic, lots of fun, and there was tons of love to go around!

My bedroom was in the basement, and it was a good size with an ensuite! Very private and...comfortable. Yes, I was very comfortable! The idea of leaving wasn't on my mind.

The time passed by so quickly! I became "Gramma Margie" to the three little ones. The young mom and I became fast friends.

I owned nothing more than a car and the few belongings that had fit into it when I left my previous home three years earlier. It wasn't my choice to begin with, but once I understood I had been living in an emotionally and verbally abusive environment, I realized leaving was for the best, although by no means easy. The hope had been that my husband would get some help just as I had chosen to, and then maybe we could reconcile and resume our marriage relationship. Sadly, his choice was to be bitter and get angrier instead. As a result,

I didn't return. Instead, I had found this very comfortable place to stay – a safe home.

In my new life, I was loved and cared for, and I cared for them. It seemed like the perfect set up. I felt so blessed and was finally at peace...something quite foreign to me.

Although I had found such a great place to live, and they were happy to have me stay there indefinitely, I began to experience a deep, gut feeling that this living arrangement wasn't meant to last much longer. I worried a bit because I had no idea how or what I would do if things were to change. I didn't have much money saved up, and what I made monthly got spent on necessities.

Now, I have learned that the tough things I have gone through in the past have schooled me in my faith. I have grown into someone with a depth and wisdom that I couldn't have received without the difficulties I have had to endure. Life's lessons are the fertilizer for good, solid growth in the Lord. I had been taught those things as a young Christian and had experienced it as I matured. I am truly grateful now. I can't say that I would want to go back to any of the circumstances the Lord brought me through, but I can say with confidence that they grew me up! I couldn't have the same depth of compassion that I now have for people experiencing difficult situations had I not gone through similar things myself!

I have learned that when things get tough, God is there. He walks with me through it all. Life doesn't necessarily get easier. In fact, it sometimes seems to get more difficult. And yet, God was and is walking with me always!

I had grown even more in my faith since living in the basement suite as I depended on God to provide for and protect me. So, with the knowledge I had acquired and this faith that I depended on, I was willing to believe God knew best. Even though I didn't know what that feeling deep in my gut meant, I gave my concerns up to Him.

That didn't stop the questions though. Where would I live? Should I be looking at apartments? Would I be able to afford the extra expenses of living on my own? Should I be looking for a roommate? What do you want me to do, Lord? I felt stuck!

When the time came, it came fast! A girlfriend had mentioned to me that maybe I should consider moving out from my basement dwelling and move on with my life. She gave me some good, solid reasons for this change, and I must say I agreed with her, but…who, what, where, and how?

Within days, I was travelling from Red Deer to Calgary for a meeting with some friends. The thought crossed my mind as I was driving, "You'll be moving to Calgary." I shrugged that idea off very quickly. I had never *ever* thought of moving to Calgary. It just wasn't on my radar. I didn't even ponder the idea, just dismissed it entirely.

During that visit in Calgary, another friend challenged me to think about why I was still living in the basement suite...and why I was feeling stuck. Odd. How did she know I was feeling stuck? But stranger still was when she boldly told me that I was being controlled by shame!

Bam! I felt like I had been knocked over! She had touched a very raw spot, but it was a sore that needed to be taken care of, and I was ready to hear it! I knew right away that she was right.

I had been staying in my safe, comfortable, basement suite because I felt ashamed. With all the things that had happened to me along with the difficulties I had experienced, shame had attached itself. I didn't feel that I deserved anything more than what I currently had. I didn't deserve my own place, nor did I think that I would ever be able to afford it. I wasn't good enough! Shame covered me like a blanket.

Now, I knew better than to believe these things. So, why was I struggling with them? Because I didn't even realize I was!

Shame is insidious and deceitful. It hides and stays hidden! That's why shame is shame. Therefore, we have a hard time acknowledging our shame because it wants to stay hidden, keeping us in bondage.

Watch out! When shame is exposed there is freedom!

It was suggested that I do some serious journaling and expose every area of shame that I could come up with. So I did! The Lord gave me several revelations that set me free from the shame that had been controlling me. Better yet, with shame gone, I discovered courage in its place! Now that's exciting!

Back to the day that the Lord shone His light on my shame... I was with the same two friends who had initially suggested that I needed to move on. I honestly can't remember how it happened, but guess what? I decided to move to Calgary. By faith, I just *knew* I was supposed to, even though I still had no idea who, what, where, or how.

I stayed over in Calgary that night pondering my new decision, excited and not the slightest bit nervous. Crazy, yes, but God was up to something good! I knew it!

The next day, my two friends and I went out for breakfast, and we were discussing the decision to move. Not only had I decided to move, but the friend from Red Deer had decided to move as well. Neither of us could give you an explanation as to why we had decided to move. By faith, we just sensed this was the direction God was taking us.

The conversation we were having was filled with excitement of what God was up to. I was prompted to ask my Calgary friend if they had ever sold the "Safe Haven" that her husband had been led by God to renovate (rebuild from the floor up). He had been told that this home was to be built for an unknown woman who had come out of an abusive situation and wanted to rebuild her life.

The answer was long and convoluted because someone had been interested in it and yet it appeared that they no longer were. My Red Deer friend and I both realized together that this could be an answer to our housing dilemma now that we were moving to Calgary. We could live together!

However, there was only one problem. This place was for sale, not for rent.

The words "The Lord will provide!" came out of my friend from Calgary's mouth very clearly. Actually, she was pretty adamant! So, it was decided! The two of us were going to buy Safe Haven! The "who, what, and where" had been revealed, but the "how" was going to be interesting because neither of us felt we could afford to buy it.

Now, this is where faith stepped in once again. In the next month while we were preparing for the move, questions haunted us. Yet, we shared our reservations with each other, and when one was weak, the other was strong. We held on to our faith that God had set this up for us and that we were meant to move ahead...and move ahead we did. Through discussions with the owners and realizing God was at work, we came up with an agreement that suited us all. A contract was signed, and within the month, we were moved in!

We knew that arriving at this quick decision was not conventional. Furthermore, we came to realize that when God reveals His plan, He expects us to step out in faith.

I have learned some things on this faith journey. First of all, God has plans for me that I haven't even conceived of yet, and they won't happen if I don't practice faith! Secondly, if I were to have let doubt enter into my thoughts to linger for any period of time, I would not be experiencing the current blessing of having a home I can call my own. Thirdly, I realize that having faith is about hoping in something that is unseen. So, I hang on tenaciously to my faith that God has a plan for my life, and He is enjoying unfolding it for me day by day! In that place, I experience His blessings daily! Yes, I falter, but God is full of grace and mercy. When I fix my eyes back on Him, I am blessed!

"For I know the plans I have for you,"
declares the Lord,
"plans to prosper you and not to harm you,
plans to give you hope and a future."
(Jeremiah 29:11, NIV)

Recently, I was looking at some photos and memorabilia when I came across a saying that intrigued me. I have no idea where it came from or who said it, but it was very timely and appropriate for me!

"Your future doesn't lie ahead of you.
It is in your mind right now!"

When I focus on the promises of God and believe in the good things He says He has in store for me, then *that* will become my future. However, if I doubt and question and think these things can't happen, they won't.

Choosing to trust God with my future has led to breakthrough in other areas. There has been such peace and joy in my heart. I find myself feeling more settled than ever before. There has also been an increase in my income. How did all these wonderful changes happen for me? I *know* faith had a lot to do with it!

Margie McIntyre is the author of *Mind Matters – Change Your Mind, Change Your Life*! and *The Last Piece of the Puzzle – Domestic Abuse.* Whether she is writing, reaching out to hurting women, or working as a financial agent helping families "make money work", she loves being a mother and a grandmother most of all.

Choose You This Day

~CHERYL REGIER~

Where does faith start? As Christians, we likely hear quite often about building or increasing our faith along with practicing or exercising that faith. But before we can do any of that, we need to know the beginning – the very foundation – of our faith.

Hebrews 11:6 states that we must first believe that God exists. The basis for life as a Christian starts with the simple belief that God IS and that He exists. Then, out of that belief, a very important decision follows. Joshua articulates what that decision is when he admonishes Israel to *"choose you this day whom ye will serve...but as for me and my house, we will serve the Lord."* (Joshua 24:15, KJV) This is the foundation – the starting point – for our faith in God. Without this choice to believe, we cannot please God or access any of the "more" that He has planned for us as believers.

Choosing God happens at the point of salvation, but it is also a *daily* exercise. Knowing this as the foundational piece to having and practicing faith is extremely important. In fact, without the daily *choice* to serve God, we cannot build our faith, never mind access mountain moving faith.

My husband and I have experienced some pretty intense trials over the past years. To tell the truth, we have been at the end of our "faith rope" many a time. In those moments, our thoughts were not about building our faith. No! Instead, we were desperate to survive just one more day, to find something, *anything* to keep our hope alive that good could come out of our trial and that God would change things for the better. For myself, this meant tapping back into my foundation for faith.

I was reading a devotional on my phone the other day. It was quoting from Joel 2:28 (ESV) where the Word of the Lord starts with, *"And it shall come to pass afterward, that I will..."* One of the insights being highlighted in that devotional was that this Word of Promise and Prophecy was being spoken to the Israelites during a time of great tragedy and distress. They had experienced defeat and famine and were being encouraged to repent and turn back to the Lord. He, in His great mercy, chose to have compassion on His people when they turned to Him. In response, He brought deliverance, restoration, and provision. However, the Promise and Prophecy of verse 28 was still left unfulfilled...and it wouldn't come to pass for roughly *900 years more* until the day of Pentecost.

I don't know about you, but I don't like to wait! I am being perfectly honest here! I receive a promise from the Lord — be it finances, other resources, restoration, healing, deliverance, etc. — and I desperately desire to see it all NOW...or in the *very* near future. Additionally, I yearn for the "big" manifestation of it...that it comes about in such a way that is obvious and huge and life changing — a *complete* turnaround.

It is difficult to wait — *in faith* — when it doesn't look like it makes sense to hold on to any hope that this "exercise" can change or produce anything. Furthermore, it can be easy to miss the blessings of God that have already been seen and realized in our lives when we feel "stuck" in the waiting for promises to be fulfilled, hanging on for dear life. This is especially true in the face of urgent needs, tragic circumstances, critical situations, and other times of distress and despair.

My husband and I have experienced the intensity of being in the place of desperate survival, a place of extreme trial that tends to sap you of your inner strength and threatens your hope for the future. Yet when we have been in that place, I made the choice to fall back on my foundation of faith – *the choice to believe (serve) God* – as my anchor. Even when I am struggling to believe that God will show up and do the impossible in my life, I *choose* to believe in Him. I *choose* to not renounce my God when what is manifesting in my life defies what I had hoped and prayed would come to pass – including the promises of God that I have been standing on and believing for. Even as my heart simultaneously cries for breakthrough, I *choose* to follow the Lord.

Renouncing my faith in God is not an option. He is my foundation. On Him, I stand. My choice to serve Him is what I turn to when the going gets tough, when the enemy is working overtime to defeat me, when the mountains are huge. As I continue to choose God daily, I *am*, in all reality, practicing my faith...and that is where the opportunity to *build* my faith begins.

Habakkuk 3:17-18 talks about being in the place of desperate need but still standing in faith. I believe that this *choice* is another step to seeing one's faith grow and be elevated. It takes the stand of *"yet I will rejoice in the Lord; I will take joy in the God of my salvation."* (ESV) Job also talks about this in Job 13:15 where he says, *"Though he slay me, yet will I trust in him..."* (NIV) The daily practice of and building of faith involves many "yet will I" moments where, in spite of all that is going wrong, in spite of the agonizing wait to see promises come to pass, the choice to believe in God and trust Him remains as the foundation for faith. And the bottom line for me is that this hope is what keeps me going! He is still my salvation, and I can trust in His timing (although it can be difficult!) – just like the Israelites had to do – despite the fact that the fulfillment of the promise is further off than I would like it to be.

It's one thing to believe IN God, but hanging on to that "faith rope" can absolutely be hard, especially when it seems like nothing is moving. Submitting to the Lord's timing is a daily choice as well. "Yet will I" moments involve not just the choice to believe but also a determination to not give up on God when discouragement comes. He is still the one in control.

The lack being experienced by Habakkuk did not deter him from standing his ground. He did not abandon faith in the crisis. Likewise, I can take heart and choose faith in spite of it all. I have come way too far to give up now!

In addition, I am standing in faith for more than just myself. The choice to be faithful in choosing faith and coming back to God – the author and finisher of our faith (Hebrews 12:2) – always blessed God's people generations afterwards. It is the same for me *and* for you. Our choice to have faith is an investment in our families and for those who come after us.

Standing firm in my choice to have faith in a GOOD God is another component that takes this foundational faith piece a little further. Hebrews 11:6 also says that God's heart is to *reward* those who diligently seek after Him. Yet, when facing the mountains in my life, it is a challenge – an extreme stretch at times – to have the faith to believe and trust that He really *will* reward my faithfulness to follow Him.

Growing my faith base means embracing the *choice* to see Him as a *good* Father no matter the circumstances currently manifesting in my life. I also have to cling to the promise that He IS a REWARDER of those who seek after Him. I won't be abandoned! I won't be rejected! He is a Giver of good gifts! (See Matthew 7:7-11) It may not look like what I envisioned, but He will walk alongside me in my journey, lovingly and with great care. This is where my hope lies...that the God of MORE deeply desires that I experience the MORE that He has for me. And that MORE is accessible by faith.

The enemy definitely loves to mess with my mind, causing me to discount what God has already done and how far I have already come. He would love for me to doubt in the goodness of who God is. I know that. Being totally transparent, I can still struggle at times with trusting that He has a good future for me (Jeremiah 29:11) when the mountains I am currently up against appear immovable and the pressure is great. Yet again, I fall back on the *choice* to believe that He IS and that He is my Rewarder – a *good* God. And no matter what is thrown at me, *yet will I* believe and have hope.

The faith walk believes that the MORE exists and that faithful service – even in the face of all the mountains of hardship and trials in the world – will be rewarded in the end. God does not lie. (See Numbers 23:19) The Israelites had to wait centuries to see the gift of the Spirit descend on them...but God was true to His Promise and fulfilled it in His timing. And before that Word came to pass, He DID indeed bless and take care of His children. I know for me, reminding myself of God's character – particularly His great love for His children (Lamentations 3:22-23) and that His heart is for us, not against us (Romans 8:31) – is my anchor in times when my reward appears to be delayed. *Yet will I!*

There is one other component to the faith walk that has been challenging me. It speaks of complete surrender – a place of complete faith "abandon" that also involves choice. It builds upon the foundation of faith and takes it beyond the "yet will I" moments of trusting in God and His plan and perfect timing. In confidence it states that "God will" – because when in relationship with Him and through His Word, we can know His character as the Giver and Rewarder, a faithful God. Nevertheless, it also confidently states at the same time that *"even if He does not"* (Read Daniel 3:16-18), the *choice* is *still* to believe in God. *Even if.* Two very potent words. Like the MercyMe song by the same name, this choice states that we choose to put our hope – our faith and trust – in God alone *even if* He doesn't save us in the way we expect.

Faith and building faith that can move mountains involves CHOICE – <u>always</u>. Choosing God is our faith's foundation. Furthermore, it chooses to declare *"yet will I"* in the face of tragedy, trauma, and trials. It chooses to surrender all by saying *"even if"* You don't, I will still follow after You. It takes a *stand of belief* in a *good* and *faithful* God.

CHOOSE YOU THIS DAY WHOM YOU WILL SERVE!

Cheryl Regier is an Editor and a #1 Best-Selling Co-Author. Her book – *Now What? A Guide Through the Editing Process* – will be released in 2018. Through her business, Zachariah House – "Editing for Impact", she serves authors as part of their publication team. She's married to a wonderful man and is mother to six amazing sons and one beautiful daughter-in-love.

He Parted the Sea for Me

~JOAN RUDDER-WARD~

"Do not be afraid. Stand still, and see the salvation of the Lord, which He will accomplish for you today..." (Exodus 14:13, NKJV)

I had to move. Again.

This was the third time in six years that I needed a place to live. I wanted my own house, but I didn't have what was needed to buy one. Here I was — a divorced woman in my late 40's, a full-time student, and unemployed – in need of a place to call home.

This all had started six years prior. My 16-year marriage had come to an end. I opted to be the one to move out of the house we had purchased and lived in for 13 years. Though it was my first home, and we had purchased it brand new, I never had the creative license to do the things I wanted to do in and around the house. My then-husband restricted what I could do, and it was only according to what he felt was appropriate. For example, pictures could not be hung on the walls because that would cause holes in the walls. Since I never really felt the house was mine, as well as to avoid an unnecessary battle, I moved out. I trusted that God would find some place for me to live along with my teenaged daughters who chose to go with me.

At this same time, I closed my photography studio. My studio, located in a strip mall, had been my haven for seven years. *This* was the place I had poured my creative energy into – through portrait sessions, darkroom work, and in decorating it. Customers would come to just sit and visit because of the 'homey' feel of the place. Ah, the studio...my place of respite from a difficult marriage. I'd go early in the morning, and many times, I'd stay until late at night. I was free to do that because my mother had moved in with us to help with my transition to full-time self-employment. She was there to prepare the meals and see after the girls when they got home from school. Though it became evident that the doors on my home and business were closing simultaneously, it didn't make the feelings of exponential loss any easier.

I had mentioned at a prayer meeting at church that I was looking for some place to move. A couple in the church told me they had a house they could rent out and offered it to me. Thank God! Answered prayer!

I decided to go back to school and finish my Bachelor's degree in business and then work towards my Master's. That was going to take a total of almost 4 years. My plan was to stay in the rental home until I finished my MBA, but after 2 years, the owners decided to sell the house. So, once again, I needed to find somewhere to live.

By this time, my then-husband and I had gone to court with regard to our divorce, and I had been awarded a small amount of alimony. Even with supplementing that alimony with income as a substitute teacher, I didn't have enough to pay for an apartment on my own. My previous landlords had been very generous in not charging me what they could have gotten for rent in order to help me out. Transitioning to a higher amount for housing was too much for me at this point.

I moved in temporarily with my mother. She was renting a home nearby and had custody of my sister's children at the time. I needed 18 more months to finish my Master's. Knowing that this arrangement was short-term, I began mapping out a plan of action for buying a home for myself. And I felt I had a solid, sensible plan: Save for a down payment. Finish degree. Find a good-paying job. Buy a house.

I started looking for a home right away during that last year. I knew what I was going to need as a down payment and how much income I would require to have what I wanted in a home. I felt that, surely, after I got my MBA, I would easily find employment with the salary I planned to make.

ON WITH THE SEARCH

Oh, "the best laid plans of mice and men!"[1] Things just didn't happen the way they were supposed to. My mother's landlord decided she was going to sell her house within a year. My mother then decided her time for raising children was ending and that she would move – alone – into a senior citizen's complex. My window of time for securing a home for myself was closing sooner than I had planned for.

TEMPTED TO MAKE A DEAL WITH THE DEVIL

The pressure was on. My sensible, well-thought-out plan was becoming null and void. The circumstances had changed before all the cards could fall in the right place. What was I going to do?

By this time, my now ex-husband had become a little more congenial. We had not yet settled on the property we jointly owned, so I proposed we leave things as they were, but that we jointly buy *another*

---

[1] Saying adapted from a line in "To a Mouse" by Robert Burns

house for me to live in with the girls. This way, I could use his income and the original house as collateral, and we'd just maintain separate residences. I would then sign off on the original house, and he would sign off on the one for me. He agreed to do that. However, after much prayer and seeking the Lord, I knew that this was NOT the way to go. I finally came to the end of myself and surrendered it all to God.

"Lord, what do you want me to do? I don't have a steady job yet, little income, and not enough money saved up yet. How is this going to work? What am I to do? Where am I to be searching?"

I felt the Lord wanted me to trust HIM to provide what I desired. HE would provide the right house for me.

This was going to be a biggie! I needed a strategy. I knew it was vital for me to have unwavering faith and to keep my focus on God and *His ability* to make what seemed impossible possible. One of my main, go-to passages of Scripture I relied on during this time was Exodus 14. This chapter recounts the story where God parted the Red Sea for the Israelites who were fleeing from their Egyptian captors. That passage of Scripture would be my rock for the days and struggles ahead. Many times, I would cry out to

God, "Lord! You parted that Red Sea of impossibility for them. Surely you will part, for me, this Red Sea that I'm facing."

FINDING THE LOCATION

A few days later, I found the area I wished to begin my search. My daughters and I were checking homes in a new development near our current residence. We struck up a conversation with a woman who was also looking through the model homes. She said she was happy that she was having a custom home built on an acre of land, and it was for less than what the homes in this particular area were selling for.

I asked her where, and she directed me to a city I had never heard of before – Hesperia. It was 50-60 miles north.

We went to check out Hesperia. It was in the High Desert...and I loved it! It was mostly rural, which was perfect for me. And so the journey began.

I found out that the city had a down payment assistance program for prospective buyers who met certain qualifications. You could get up to $20,000 interest-free for a down payment that you would begin paying back after 15 years. Though I didn't have a regular, full-time job, I had steady income, and that income fell within the guidelines. I had to go through a process of qualifying, and several times, glitches came up that had the potential to jeopardize my taking advantage of this opportunity. Yet, as I steadily prayed, trusted, and believed God, I could pray with confidence that things would go through the way they should. There were times when I would have to focus on the wonder of Exodus 14. I would say to the Lord, "God, You did this for them, and I know You're going to part that Red Sea for me." Finally, everything was done and approved, and I was given the wonderful news that I qualified for $20,000, the maximum available for a down payment.

Next, I had to find a house that fit within a certain price range. After a couple of months of searching, I found the perfect house – a lovely, corner-lot home on ¾ of an acre. Yay! I was envisioning right away the huge vegetable and flower garden I always dreamed of having.

The sellers accepted my offer, and so escrow began. Escrow is where things can really get dicey. No one wants to have a house 'fall out of escrow'. A couple of issues did come up during the escrow process, but I kept looking to God, trusting Him to bring things through. And He did.

I also had a prayer partner to pray with me on a weekly basis about the house situation. This was a strategy I put in place as I looked to God to do things His way and overcome any difficulties.

While the process of escrow was going on, other outside things were happening as well that threatened my peace and focus. Unfortunately, when you're moving forward, there may be people who, when they should be cheering you on, are releasing opposition instead. There were one or two such individuals who made a point of letting me know that they didn't think that this was the place I should move to, or they didn't think this was the right time, or...whatever. Sometimes, such opposition is just plain jealousy. During this time, I had to be on guard against such distractions to my faith and focus.

Escrow did close. I got my keys and moved into my new home. *My* home – the home the Lord made possible for ME.

I never did get that full-time, salaried job that I was banking on to make this happen. No. The Lord's plan was for me to restart my business in a new area and also to serve as a substitute teacher for a new school district. HE provided the perfect home that helped me move forward towards the purposes He had for my life and my future.

MY THREE TAKEAWAYS

Have a faith-building strategy. I had my go-to, miracle event (Exodus 14) as my point of reference when I needed a boost to keep my faith up. I also had a prayer partner to be in agreement with me throughout the process.

Be careful of who you share with while working towards your miracle. Not everyone needs to know what you're doing. Some may release negativity into the atmosphere that you will have to fight off and resist. This can seriously dampen your faith. Instead, ask God whom you can trust to share with.

Don't stop praying, believing, and confessing until the keys are in your hand. See it through to completion. Don't let 'almost there' stop you from forcefully exercising your faith.

Joan Rudder-Ward is a storyteller, photographic artist, and filmmaker. She is the producer of the weekly TV broadcast, *Silver Sage* (ASilverSage.com), and founder of the Positive Image Network (PhotographyWithPurpose.com). She is the author of the upcoming book, *Picture Perfect: Becoming All You Were Created to Be.*

Perspective and Trust

~RUTH STACY, PSY.D.~

When I think of a mountain, I think of the huge amount of dirt, rocks, debris, trees, inclement weather, and forces of nature that have shaped that mountain over thousands of years. Some mountains are taller than others and some mountains are more beautiful than others. One thing is for sure – each mountain always looks bigger up-close than from a distance. The up-close view is when we are at the base of the mountain staring up at it, and the distant view is when we see it from miles away where it looks small, even minute.

Spiritually speaking, two different perspectives are involved when we consider the mountain we are facing. The up-close perspective is our perspective. The distant perspective is God's perspective.

The up-close perspective focuses on the size of the mountain and the enormous problem facing you. It is the moment of: "Oh, my gosh! Dare I trust God to accomplish this in my life?" This view stares at the mountain wondering how the problem or situation will be solved. It considers only what it sees at the moment...not the larger picture.

Sometimes when life is tough, when we receive shocking news, or when we experience a traumatic event, that's all we can see in the moment. When staring up at the mountain, it is easy to forget about everything else except the mountain in front of us. It is hard to fathom a bigger picture when the enormous is so up close and personal.

The distant view, however, considers the larger picture. It considers the resources needed or available to help solve the problem, the people who need to be involved in the process, those who should be excluded from the process, the strategy to address the problem, and the timing to implement the strategy. All this and more involves the distant perspective that takes in the whole picture.

I recently visited some friends who live where it snows. While driving to go see them, it started snowing hard, and it was an act of nail-biting faith for me to continue driving. I had to overcome a fear of driving in blowing snow – a fear that was created as a result of a harrowing experience I'd had years ago.

Several years ago, I was caught in a snowstorm while driving in the mountains where there was almost zero visibility. I was on a narrow, two-lane highway with a drop off on both sides. There was *no* room for error, and there was *no* place to pull over to wait the storm out. I could not stop in the middle of the road either as cars behind me could run into me due to the poor visibility. I prayed in the spirit as I fought back the terror that gripped me as I drove.

I occasionally saw a semi truck that I thought I could follow. However, I could not keep up with the semi trucks. I even had semi trucks pass me. These trucks were able to go faster as their heavy weight gave them better traction. They also had better visibility because the truck driver sat up higher and could see over obstacles that hindered my view, such as other cars. In addition, these big trucks had special running lights that my car did not have. The special running lights gave the truck drivers better visibility and increased the distance that they could see.

After what seemed to be an eternity, one semi truck slowed down, allowing me to follow it to safety. I followed it for several miles until there was a rest area where I could stop and wait out the storm. When I turned into the rest area, the semi truck sped up and continued to its destination.

I spent the rest of the night at the rest area with several other cars that were parked there to wait out the storm. It was extremely cold. I only had my coat. Unfortunately, I did not have any emergency supplies with me such as food, water, or blankets to keep warm. The rest area had restrooms and water, and that was it. Occasionally, I turned on the car to warm up, but I had to be careful, for I was low on gas.

The next morning when the weather cleared, and it was light outside, I continued my journey. Much to my surprise, two miles down the road was a motel on the edge of the town where I had planned to spend the night. Another couple miles after that, there was a gas station and places to eat. Within just five miles from the rest area where I had stopped, there was every provision that I needed – a warm bed, food, and gas. Only five miles away.

When I stopped at the rest area, I had no idea how close I was to town and all that I needed to be safe, warm, and provided for. Did I feel upset and second-guess my decision to stop at the rest stop? At the moment, absolutely not! I had gone as far as I thought I could go, and I was so thankful that I had made it to the rest area.

Looking back now, though, I can't help but wonder what if I had passed up the rest area and continued to follow the semi-truck. The semi truck did not signal me, flash its lights, or give me any indication to stop at the rest area. That was my choice. I did so thinking it was my only option to safety. My fear is what stopped me from going any farther.

What if I had trusted the truck driver a little bit longer and gone those few extra miles to town? How much different my experience would have been!!! How much better would it have been to follow the semi-truck to safety and provision rather than stopping prematurely, just short of my destination? Plus, the experience created a fear of driving in snow that I would have to conquer later.

I had operated with the up-close perspective, one that was focused strictly on the problem facing me. The truck driver, however, could see farther ahead. Along with his knowledge of the road, he had the distant, long-term view.

This is similar to our relationship with God. How often do we settle for the close-up view of the problem or situation rather than trusting God with the larger picture? How often do we settle for something less than what God has for us simply because we cannot trust Him to lead us a little bit farther? How often do we settle for anger, disillusionment, or pain rather than trusting God enough to allow Him into that area that so desperately needs to be healed? How many times do we turn a deaf ear to wise counsel from others simply because we are afraid to trust a little bit longer?

Yes, I should have been better prepared for driving in winter weather. And yes, I should have listened to the weather forecast before driving to my destination. This could have prevented me getting caught in the snowstorm and being put in such a dangerous situation. God in His mercy used the truck driver to lead me. But again, I wonder what would have happened if I had exercised the courage and trust to follow the truck driver a little bit farther.

What if God is the "truck driver" wanting to lead me into the next phase for my life? Do I step out in faith and trust Him to lead me to the destination He has for me? Or, out of fear, do I stop prematurely and miss His blessing and provision? Do I stay stuck on the close-up view and my perspective of a situation? Or do I adopt God's view – the larger perspective – and rely on what He sees for my future? I must make this choice daily.

How about you? Are you stuck on the close-up view of the mountain you are facing? Or are you willing to adopt God's perspective of the situation?

Proverbs 3:5-6 (NASB) states: *"Trust in the Lord with all your heart and do not lean on your own understanding. In all your ways acknowledge Him, and He will make your paths straight."*

I encourage you to examine your journey of life, not with condemnation or regrets but to prayerfully consider where to go from here. Prayerfully examine what areas of life God desires to take you farther, to make your paths straight. Trust Him to lead you that little bit farther and don't stop at the rest area. It may feel safe, but to go those few extra miles leads you to greater blessing, provision, and true safety. I encourage you not to settle for less or second best but to allow God to lead you to a greater depth of healing, direction, and purpose.

Trust in God and His perspective – the bigger picture! It will help you navigate the mountains you face in life and take you to the next level.

Dr. Ruth Stacy, a licensed clinical psychologist, is a #1 best-selling author who longs to see people healed and set free from those things that hold them back from living life to the fullest and fulfilling the call of God on their lives. Be watching for her latest book, *Pocketful of Gratitude*, which will be available on Amazon very soon.

Faith

Supernatural Joy in Sorrow

~LEE-ANNE TYERMAN~

The Greek word for "joy" when referring to the Fruit of the Spirit is *Chara*. It describes an inner feeling of gladness, delight, or rejoicing that is independent of what is "happening" as it is based on spiritual realities and not what is going on in the natural. This type of joy – a supernatural joy – comes only from God and the Holy Spirit. This spiritual source of joy will strengthen you through your trials.

I was overcome with supernatural joy such as I have never experienced before in my life as I sat at my mom's funeral. I could not wipe the joy off of my face! Sounds strange, I know, but I knew without a doubt that she was in heaven – at peace at last. The events leading up to her passing along with the how He orchestrated the details of her funeral increased my faith that God is real and that He cares for us. Despite the sadness of my mom's death, my joy overflowed at God's faithfulness.

The news came that my mom had lung cancer. Many years of smoking had taken a toll on her body. She had the cancer removed from her lungs, which gave her five more years of life. After five years, however, the cancer came back, and this time, it was all through her body. The diagnosis was extremely grim.

Yet, my greatest concern was her salvation. A recent convert myself, I began to earnestly pray for her salvation. On my next trip home to see my mom, it was imperative that I share the Gospel with her.

The Gospel is the message of hope for eternal life in heaven because Jesus Christ sacrificed His life on the cross for our sins. If we ask Jesus to forgive us and ask Him into our lives, we receive the salvation gift.

When I got home to Windsor, Ontario, I invited the pastor from the Alliance church to visit my mom and I. During that meeting, she accepted the Gospel message of forgiveness and eternal life. What joy and peace filled my heart! This increased my faith in God. I had proof that He answers prayer.

Lamentations 3:22-23 – *It is of the Lord's mercies that we are not consumed, because his compassions fail not. They are new every morning: great is thy faithfulness.* (KJV)

A few days later, I asked my mom if she wanted to go to the St. Aiden's Anglican Church on the next

Sunday. She answered, "Yes." What a privilege to attend church with my mom! I hadn't seen her attend church since I was a little girl about 30 years earlier. That Sunday, we took communion together. It was like "coming home". Again, I felt such supernatural joy. This increased my faith that He was directing my steps even through my mom's terminal illness.

When we took communion, my mom and I recognized the lay minister. He had worked at the Walkerville post office with my mom for many years. Maybe he had prayed for her or witnessed to her at work those many years ago. I will never know. We also saw somebody at the church who had been beside her in the hospital when she was first diagnosed. There are no coincidences with God. These reconnections were the Lord surrounding my mom with His faithfulness.

Within a few months, my mom's condition worsened, and she ended up in the hospital. This time, she would not leave. One night, my mom's friend of 50 years, Irish Jobin, sat outside her hospital room during a visit. Lo and behold, the lay minister from the Anglican Church passed by the room. He stopped and asked Irish whom she was visiting. She responded that it was my mom. Later, he came by and visited my mom before he left the hospital, ministering to her before she died.

Ephesians 3:20 – *Now to Him who is able to do exceedingly abundantly above all that we ask or think...* (NKJV)

In her last days, God surrounded my mom with divine connections of love and comfort. The reconnection with the Anglican pastor was especially God-ordained. Even though she hadn't been to church in over 30 years, God brought this man who had known her personally to minister to her. He even arranged for a guitar player to come and play music for her while she was in her hospital bed. My older sister along with a few others who were there sang songs around my mom, holding hands. During that beautiful time together with the pastor and the musician, the Spirit was present. My sister said that she could really feel His Presence in the room. The Comforter truly ministered to my mom in her last days.

For my mom's funeral, the Anglican minister was also asked to officiate. During the service, he brought forth the message of forgiveness to family members and friends left behind so that they could be set free as well.

Through the gift of salvation, my mom was set free indeed. Despite a time dealing with a terminal illness, God came alongside her and I in special and unexpected ways. Could I have ever imagined that God would take care of every detail for the care of my mom before she died? Could I have ever imagined that He loved her enough to set up the circumstances for her celebration of life during her funeral service? Furthermore, He gave me supernatural joy in a time of sorrow. God was, and IS, so faithful!

God's faithfulness continued. About a month later, my one older sister called me up. This was the same sister who was so touched by the Spirit during that time of singing for my mom in the hospital. In our conversation, she accepted the Lord over the phone. Supernatural joy overflowed once again! I was *so* excited, I just had to go outside and jump on the trampoline in my backyard to celebrate my sister's salvation!

I hope this testimony will increase your faith that you can and will receive supernatural joy even in your trials when you trust in God. Please, never give up hope and keep praying by faith. Wait with expectancy that God will do far more than you could ever ask or think!

Lee-Anne Tyerman has worked in the mental health and addiction field for nine years. She is blessed with a wonderful family – a son, his wife, a daughter, and five grandchildren.

The Essence of Faith

~RUTH YESMANISKI~

"...when the Son of Man comes, will he find faith on the earth?" - Luke 18:8b (NIV)

"Faith is the bird that sings while it is yet dark." - Max Lucado

When challenged with the writing of this chapter for *Walking In Your Destiny – Building Faith That Can Move Mountains*, I must admit that I felt overwhelmed, unequipped, as though I had nothing of noteworthiness to contribute to such a powerful theme. I took a cursory look at where I am at in the present moment. At first glance, I believe the best description of my life is that of being in a desert – "a dry and thirsty land" – bordering on despair and hopelessness at times. I have been groping around in "the dark" with only sparks or faint glimmers of light breaking through. What do I have to 'sing' about?

I could go on in explaining this place where loneliness overtakes my thoughts, when it seems like the world conspires to rob me of everything, *especially* my joy. But each time I find myself at what I perceive to be my 'bottom', the remembrance of where I have come from and the fact that I am still alive and able to write this excerpt is evidence to me that I have a God who knows me. 'Something' within my spirit responds.

Let me ask you, my dear reader...where does 'faith' actually begin in a person's life? I'm not necessarily talking about faith in God but the essence of faith.

I believe that faith is inherent in our make-up, our DNA, our humanness. Even before we are totally cognizant of it, we, as babies, have faith that we will be cared for by our parents. We have faith that, when we cry out, our mothers or caregivers will pick us up and care for whatever our immediate need is. 'Something' in our make-up is designed to trust that our needs will be met.

As children develop in a loving and nurturing environment, natural expectations of trust emerge. When we begin to talk and to walk, we practice an inherent faith that our parents will be there to teach us ways to communicate and catch us when we fall. As we continue to grow, our nature wants to trust that our caregivers will provide for each and every need along with giving us access to learning and opportunities as we mature. We develop faith that our parents will help us through the tough periods of growing up, they will protect us from evil and dangers that may be around us, guarding us from those who may wish to do us harm. We learn to trust that they have our best interests at heart, no matter what, because we are their children. We exercise faith in their love for us. Even though their love is not a tangible 'thing', we see the outward manifestation of that love through their actions and provision for us.

This inherent beginning to faith tells me that 'something' in our core is designed to respond to the nurture and care of a God – our Heavenly Father – who loves us. In this truth, the essence of faith exists. But due to the nature of a fallen world, that essence of faith can be 'lost'. Life happens, and various negative events and experiences can work against what is in our DNA to respond to a loving God.

I was taught about Jesus as a young girl. My parents decided that my sisters and I should start going to a Sunday School in the neighborhood in which we lived. Although my parents themselves did not attend unless it was a very special event, they felt that it would be a good thing for us, primarily because of their own upbringing in church in our country of origin. It was during my Sunday School years that I accepted Jesus as Lord and Saviour.

I was always in awe of the Sunday School teachers I had. I especially admired their strength of faith and how they were concerned about our salvation. We were taught that Christ was gentle, loving, and wanted us to give our lives to Him. However, we were also taught that God is a God of wrath, He is a judging God, and we must flee from any wickedness in our lives. And yet... God was one with Jesus... and with the Holy Spirit... and Jesus was one with God the Father *and* the Holy Spirit. In a sense, I realize where some of my confusion arose as a child. I believe this conflicting picture and my immature perception of God – with no spiritual understanding or insight – was the cause of a lot of wrong choices throughout my early adulthood.

Life went on, and I graduated from high school. I spent a year in Europe trying to "find myself" and to figure out what I should choose as a life path. After my return, I stepped away from the church.

I moved to a new city to attend college, but upon trying to get back into a church near my residence, there seemed to be a coldness in the atmosphere that had me walk away on a spiritual detour for over ten years. During that time, I met and married a young man with whom I share two children. However, the marriage did not last. This was largely due to not having a solid foundation of faith to build upon.

I know I was lost because I lacked the spiritual nourishment I needed to thrive and build my life upon. Without spiritual nourishment, your soul withers. Although you can fill your life with times and events and people that bring pleasure to your physical being, when you are alone – in the quiet of your mind and your inner being – the emptiness is a constant void. A quote that is paraphrased from Blaise Pascal's *Pensées* says it most eloquently: "There is a God-shaped vacuum in the heart of every man which cannot be filled by any created thing, but only by God, the Creator, made known through Jesus Christ." Truthfully, I had forgotten the essence of faith.

I met my second husband during a time where I was close to ending it all because I just didn't know where else to turn. Although I continued to believe in my Creator (God) and in Jesus and therefore I knew that I couldn't take my own life, I felt that I had lost my chance at a relationship with Him because of my 'wrong' choices. But God is so good! He continues to chase us even when we aren't aware of it!

Through a recovery program that my second husband introduced me to, and especially through a book that he gave me to read, *In Tune with the Infinite* by Ralph Waldo Trine, my perception of God began to change. In Ralph Waldo Trine's book, the author explains the love of God in such a way that it changed my heart knowledge to that of understanding that, although He was a God of vengeance and wrath in the Old Testament, with the coming of Christ, He showed us that He IS a God of love, mercy, and grace. Thus, began my journey back to the essence of faith and what was inherently within me that could respond to this good God.

Although my husband and I had our highs and lows and our ups and downs during our 25-year marriage, the anchor for me was that Christ was the center of our marriage. We were a triangle, and we went into our marriage with that understanding. During these years, I believe that God was building my faith reserve, strengthening me in my understanding of my connection with Him and that it was also a personal thing. My husband and I did not always share the same strength of faith, nor did we always live out our lives the way we should have or model the ideal, faith-based partnership, but we continued to try.

On September 15, 2011, my faith was shaken to the core!

Six days earlier, we were told my husband had lung cancer...inoperable...and that he only had a few weeks to live. One day earlier, we had a consult with the doctors, and they gave us an even shorter timeline, so we started planning on bringing my husband home for the remaining time. That evening, I said goodbye, expecting to spend the next day with him at the hospital along with our oldest son. As we were getting dressed and prepared to go to the hospital early on the 15th, I received a phone call from the hospital requesting us to come immediately as there had been an event that happened overnight.

When we got to his room, we found that my husband was unresponsive and having difficulty breathing. The hospital staff was very gentle and cautious when they advised us that he was in his last hours. By 3 o'clock in the afternoon, his spirit had left his body.

It was difficult for me to pray during the next days. I truly struggled, wondering why God would take him before I even had a chance to say goodbye – to ask forgiveness for when I had failed him and to sort practical things out – to be able to wrap my head around what I needed to do. In the days that followed, I found it particularly difficult knowing that Jesus was sitting on the right hand of God the Father and my husband was with them...but I was here alone, not knowing how to carry on.

Since then, I have had my eyes opened up to a whole new realm of spiritual awareness. Holy Spirit moved me out of the church I had attended for 19 years and planted me in a church where I experienced what can best be described as my perception of what the early Christians experienced in their gatherings. The journey has been an adventure to say the least! At times, it feels like I am on the edge of a precipice, not knowing whether I will make it another day in the natural, but inevitably, God is there to lift me up.

In my own intellect, I have no way to explain the faith that is still alive in me, even when I fail God through poor choices or wrong turns. Nevertheless, it is the assurance that He loves me, and He will not allow the enemy to prevail, that keeps me believing that a better day is coming. I keep coming back to the essence or core of my faith – that which was placed within me even at birth – that enables me to respond to His love and have faith that my needs will be met.

I am reminded in Scripture of what Jesus said in John 16:33 (NIV): *"...In this world you will have trouble. But take heart! I have overcome the world."* It seems to me that I am in the crucible of 'trouble', praying that the refining that needs to happen will indeed happen according to His promise.

I also believe that God has a plan and a purpose for my life. I can 'go out into the world' and be a light in the darkness. I have a testimony of how He is bringing me through and *has* brought me through this 'desert' experience into a flourishing land, not only with a deeper and more abiding faith, but with tangible examples of His goodness in all areas of my life. This can be used as an encouragement to many who yearn to build faith during dark times.

The thought I want to leave you with, dear reader, is this:

Faith is the assurance that despite how we fail or feel, God has an enduring love for us. He loves us no matter what. Deep within our very being, God planted the seed – the essence of what is needed – to have faith in that love.

How will you respond???

Ruth Yesmaniski is a #1 Best-Selling Co-Author and in the process of writing her first book. She has been in the accounting field for most of her career and is now involved in Book Shepherding and editing of books. She is the mother of 4 adult sons and has 8 (soon to be 9) grandchildren.

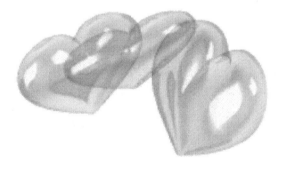

Called To Write

~KATHLEEN D. MAILER~

You are reading this chapter because YOU KNOW - you ARE CALLED to 'WRITE' THAT BOOK!

Perhaps you said to yourself, "Gee, these chapters are amazing! I think I would have something to contribute here! I could write something like this!" If that is you, you are in the right place.... Please read on, dear friend. I have some advice for you in my own story.

Isn't it time you turned the page, and started a NEW chapter in your life?

When it comes to getting that book out of your head and into the hands of the people that need it, it can be frustrating, overwhelming, and seemingly impossible.

I know how you feel! On writing my very first book almost 20 years ago, I ran into every scenario you can think of!

I spent too much money because I didn't have someone to show me the most effective way for the best price. I literally spent tens of thousands of dollars to get that first book published! However, I don't regret it! Why? Because **every cent I**

invested into that book came back to me more than 1000-fold (not a joke!).

I spent too much time fighting with what I lovingly refer to as, my Inner Terrorist™. You know the 'guy' in your head that tells you; "You're not smart enough!" "You're not good enough." "Do you know how many business books there are out there?" "Seriously, you didn't get high enough marks in English to pull a book off." "Blah, blah, blah…"

As a matter of fact this fight within myself left me with devastating consequences. I wanted desperately to show my Dad my book. I was one week too late. **Yet, I learned that life was too short to sit on my dreams. I never made that mistake again.** I made a vow –as I dug a hole in his fresh grave to 'plant' the book – that I wouldn't let my negative self-talk ever hold me back to this degree again! I would share with the world the truth of who they are in Christ – so that they can let go of self-deprecating behaviors.

Yes, writing a book can cause such a massive shift in our own personal world – but do you know what else I found? It can make a huge impact on those important people that YOU are CALLED to influence – for God's Glory with YOUR STORY!

It is because of MY PERSONAL testimony of tears and triumphs that I started helping authors just like you get that book out of their head and into the hands of the people that need it. I have taught tens of thousands of people over the years everything I could about writing a book, publishing it with ease, and how to make money right away to get a return on their investment. You guessed it, that was when "A Book is Never A Book" Boot Camp was born...

WHAT MAKES THIS BOOT CAMP SO DIFFERENT?
When it comes to Christians writing and publishing their books, many find that the devil sends confusion and chaos to stop them from reaching out with their POWERFUL MESSAGE to make an impact for the Kingdom.

We find that **many don't even know where to start in the process.** Over and over they start their book and then find themselves going down a bunny trail. It can be very frustrating to say the least! Besides that, there are so many places to find information these days, how do you discern what is right and true? Our "A Book is Never A Book" Boot Camp welcomes the Holy Spirit to guide us as we take you through a proven, reliable method to help bring clarity on which book you should write first - for the right reasons!
We know how hard it is to keep up the balance between God, family, and work - let alone adding a book to your 'family business'. Throughout the

event - we are skilled at showing you how to lead yourself through the process AND also giving you the extra incentive as to whom you should have as your Book Shepherd (including marketing plans) through the twists and turns of being an Author-Preneur.

You can go to our website to download the information booklet and to register:
www.ABookIsNeverABook.com

In the meantime, let me show you what to expect ....
In this 3-day, Holy-Spirit filled, hands-on, roll-up-your-sleeves event, you will:
1. Learn how to **WRITE that Book**!
2. Self-**PUBLISH it with ease**; avoiding major and expensive pitfalls and mistakes
3. **Make MONEY** while you are doing it; understanding that marketing STARTS BEFORE you write it, and
4. **BECOME a PUBLISHED AUTHOR**, by submitting your homework. You will walk out of the Boot Camp a Co-Author of our #1 Best Selling Series - *Walking In Your Destiny*™

You will also know how to use that Co-Authored book to create cash flow, open up speaking engagements, and give you credibility to **walk onto the platform to your purpose.**

'The HELL you have been through is the platform to your purpose!' *Kathleen D. Mailer*

WHAT'S MY INVESTMENT?
The better question is, "How much is it costing you to sit on your book?"
How many times has God nudged you to move forward and get it done?

How many times have you walked away from a God-given platform and left money on the table because you didn't have your book to sell as a back-end source of income?

How many event planners pass you over because your story doesn't have continued substance for their audience to solidify what they learned that day?

How many clients are going to your competition because they have a book - and you do not?

Is your message being watered down and not as effective as it can be to reach the lost for Christ because you haven't 'purposefully packaged' the POWER of your TESTIMONY?

NOT having your book available today may already be costing you a great deal!

YOU ARE CALLED TO, 'WRITE THAT BOOK!' LET'S DO IT TOGETHER!
We would love to see you at next year's boot camp.
Come and visit us at:
www.ABookIsNeverABook.com

Check out what some of our authors are saying.

DOWNLOAD your 3 FREE VIDEOS – at www.ChristianAuthorsGetPaid.com that will help you WRITE that Book! PUBLISH with Ease! And Make MONEY Now!

Please feel free to connect with us:
FB and IG @KathleenAndDanMailer
Twitter: KathleenAndDan
Website: www.KathleenAndDanMailer.com
www.ChristianAuthorsGetPaid.com
www.ABookIsNeverABook.com

But most importantly, PRAY – pray about being at the Boot Camp so we can help you –
Get clear on your message for your book; learn to write it easily; how to package it professionally;
And how to make money WHILE you are doing it.

May God bless you richly,

Kathleen Mailer

INTERNATIONAL BUSINESS EVANGELIST

Our Featured

Author's and Books

take your event to the next level book NOW!

CHRISTIANAUTHORSGETPAID.com

Enjoy some of our
other **#1 Best Selling
Books**. They are
AVAILABLE NOW
on Amazon.com

BULK ORDER
AVAILABLE NOW
Contact Our Office TODAY!

Buy in Bulk for your NEXT Event
587-333-5127
AuroraPublishing@shaw.ca

POWER UP
QUARTERLY PLANNER
for Kingdom Health Centres

POWER UP
QUARTERLY PLANNER
for Kingdom Health Centres

The Kingdom-Preneur Show
WITH KATHLEEN MAILER

www.KathleenMailer.com

> #1 Best Selling Author;
> International Business Evangelist;
> Co-Founder, Iron Sharpens Iron Ministries;
> Founder/Facilitator of "A Book Is
Never A Book" Boot Camp;
> CEO of ChristianAuthorsGetPaid.com

CALL NOW

to **ORDER BOOKS** or
to **BOOK KATHLEEN**
to SPEAK at your
next event

403-587-3127
getbooked@shaw.ca

WALKING IN THE WAKE OF THE HOLY SPIRIT

GETTING DOWN TO THE BUSINESS OF MINISTRY

Margie McIntyre

#1 Best Selling Author, Speaker, Mentor & Coach

You ARE An Overcomer.
Time to Live Life to the Fullest!

To ORDER BOOKS
or to **BOOK MARGIE**
for your next event,

403-597-0216
margiemcintyre2011@gmail.com

www.mindmattersseries.com

Latest Book
Devil, Take Your
Hands OFF
My Man!

#1 Best Selling Author
Speaker, Trainer
Founder & Facilitator of
"Winning The War On Divorce"
Coaching Program

**To ORDER BOOKS or
to BOOK SUZANNE
to speak at your next event:**

Suzanne D. Jubb
403-396- 0572
info@suzannejubb.com
www.SuzanneJubb.com

Connect with us today to
ORDER BOOKS or to
INVITE CATHY
TO SPEAK
at your next event.

#1 Best Selling Author,
Speaker, Blogger

CathyHorning.com
Cathy@CathyHorning.com

Author, Speaker, Trainer, Coach

Connect with Us Now
to ORDER BOOKS
or to INVITE
DR. RUTH STACY
to SPEAK at your
next event.

Pocketful of
Gratitude

DR. RUTH STACY

RuthStacy.com
909-359-0455
Info@RuthStacy.com

"A Book is NEVER a Book! It is so much more.

Never do you just write a book for the sake of writing it - it is a catalyst of change geared for future revenue streams you didn't even know existed!"

- Kathleen D. Mailer

www.ABookIsNeverABook.com

Zachariah House

"Editing for Impact"

Cheryl Regier, a published author as well as an editor, is dedicated to delivering high-quality editing services through Zachariah House, her business ministry of helps and service.

She provides editing for books – specializing in non-fiction, faith-based books – as well as articles, brochures, websites, and more.

Approaching each manuscript/project from two perspectives – one, of addressing the mechanics and structure of the work, and two, looking at it through the eyes of a reader – her services result in an excellent, finished product.

Cheryl works diligently to enhance each author's message and voice for the greatest impact!

For more information, please contact her at:

zachariahhouseofhelps@gmail.com

YourStoryYourLegacy@gmail.com

Ruth Yesmaniski

BOOK SHEPHERD

(403) 862-6345

Editing & Co-operative
Publishing Services for

CHRISTIANAUTHORSGETPAID.com

FOR ALL OF YOUR EDITING NEEDS

ASK ME

about your special coupon for

editing services IF you

are a partner of

ChristianAuthorsGetPaid.com

yourstoryyourlegacy@gmail.com

95416298R00089

Made in the USA
Columbia, SC
09 May 2018